PRAISE FOR
A REAL GOOD LIFE

"When I first met Sazan and Stevie about five years ago, Sazan and I were doing something together for her podcast and my skincare line. We were shooting at their home near LA, so I got an instant peek inside their private life. What struck me most was their commitment to each other and their family and faith—with some cheesy dad jokes thrown in by Stevie. With their new book, *A Real Good Life*, they explore the fundamental elements that contribute to a good life. It's an engaging and enlightening read that will empower readers to make positive changes and embrace a life of purpose."

—Cindy Crawford, model, philanthropist,
and founder of Meaningful Beauty

"A profound and inspiring book, *A Real Good Life* offers a roadmap to living a meaningful and purposeful life. The authors' thoughtful guidance will transform how you approach happiness and personal growth."

—Michael Hyatt, *New York Times* bestselling author

"*A Real Good Life* is honest, refreshing, and real. Sazan and Stevie do such a great job at giving readers a fresh perspective on happiness and success, offering something more meaningful than the hustle culture of chasing what the world says success is. An absolute must-read!"

—Carlos and Alexa PenaVega, actors and
authors of *What If Love Is the Point?*

"Prepare to be inspired starting the minute you open this book! Sazan and Stevie are personally cultivating a life they love, and they want to share those insights and wisdom with the world! *A Real Good Life* is full of amazing storytelling and encouragement for weary souls who are looking for happiness and joy!"

—Jamie Ivey, host of *The Happy Hour with Jamie Ivey* podcast

"Sazan and Stevie are two of the most genuine, intentional people I know. I respect the wisdom and honesty they share in *A Real Good Life* of their own experience in the often-glorified grind for success and hustle. It challenged me to observe my own pace and my own daily intention, and it offers validation and tangible steps on how to redefine true fulfillment. Not to mention, it's just a fun read!"

—Lauren Scruggs Kennedy, lifestyle blogger, author, and cofounder of the LSK Foundation

A REAL GOOD LIFE

A REAL GOOD LIFE

DISCOVER *the* SIMPLE MOMENTS
that BRING JOY,
CONNECTION, *and* LOVE

SAZAN AND STEVIE HENDRIX

NELSON
BOOKS
An Imprint of Thomas Nelson

Published in Nashville, Tennessee, by Nelson Books, an imprint of Thomas Nelson. Nelson Books and Thomas Nelson are registered trademarks of HarperCollins Christian Publishing, Inc.

The authors are represented by Alive Literary Agency, www.aliveliterary.com.

Thomas Nelson titles may be purchased in bulk for educational, business, fundraising, or sales promotional use. For information, please email SpecialMarkets@ThomasNelson.com.

Unless otherwise noted, Scripture quotations are taken from the Holy Bible, New International Version®, NIV®. Copyright © 1973, 1978, 1984, 2011 by Biblica, Inc.® Used by permission of Zondervan. All rights reserved worldwide. www.Zondervan.com. The "NIV" and "New International Version" are trademarks registered in the United States Patent and Trademark Office by Biblica, Inc.®

Scripture quotations marked MSG are taken from THE MESSAGE. Copyright © 1993, 2002, 2018 by Eugene H. Peterson. Used by permission of NavPress. All rights reserved. Represented by Tyndale House Publishers, a division of Tyndale House Ministries.

ISBN 978-1-4002-4075-3 (HC)
ISBN 978-1-4002-4078-4 (eBook)

Library of Congress Control Number: 2023015375

Printed in the United States of America

23 24 25 26 27 LBC 5 4 3 2 1

To our parents and grandparents whose courage and love gave us a chance for a better life, and to our three beautiful children, thank you for your patience while we wrote this book.

CONTENTS

Introduction: A Good Life   xi

MORNING: REFLECT   1

Chapter 1:   Reflect on Your Intention   5
Chapter 2:   Reflect on Your Pace   17
Chapter 3:   Reflect on Your Worth   31
Chapter 4:   Reflect on What You Say to Yourself   43

MIDDAY: FOCUS   57

Chapter 5:   Focus on Opening Your Eyes to See   61
Chapter 6:   Focus on Getting Comfortable with Chaos   71
Chapter 7:   Focus on Refusing to Avoid Your Problems   81
Chapter 8:   Focus on Goodness in Hopeless Moments   95

EVENING: GATHER   105

Chapter 9:   Find Your People and Gather   107
Chapter 10: Disconnect to Connect and Gather   117
Chapter 11: Show Up and Gather   127
Chapter 12: Grieve, Celebrate, and Gather   139

NIGHTTIME: REST   151

Chapter 13: Rest in Being Enough   153
Chapter 14: Rest in Setting Out Your Seed   161
Chapter 15: Rest in Surrendering   169
Chapter 16: Rest in Freedom   179
Chapter 17: Rest in Believing   193

Conclusion: Be Present   203
A Real Good Life Playlist   211
Acknowledgments   213
Notes   217
About the Authors   219

INTRODUCTION

A Good Life

The first day I (Sazan) laid eyes on Stevie Hendrix, he was wearing the wrong shade of foundation. I could see it from across the room.

Okay, let me back up a bit.

It was the spring of 2011. I was a student producer in the radio, television, and media department at the University of North Texas in Denton (Go Eagles!). I was ready to power through all my requirements and wrap up my degree program because Los Angeles and the entertainment industry were calling my name, and I was ready to head west.

As part of my degree program at UNT, I helped produce the weekly campus newscast. We rotated through a roster of students who were each scheduled for their turn in front of the camera to showcase their newscasting, sportscasting, or meteorology chops. In my experience, these production days often took way too long as all the news wannabes joked, postured, rewrote their copy, and worked off their nervousness all through the vehicle of Wasting My Time.

Today, I was in no mood to play.

So as I moved to my seat to begin the production meeting, I focused on telegraphing to the assembled crew that we needed to knock out this meeting and get into the studio. I let my eyes bounce around the room to see the talent on deck for the week, and that's when I noticed Stevie prepping for his sports report. Clean-shaven, necktie slightly crooked, blue eyes snapping, looking like an adorable, large twelve-year-old.

With a face spackled in a pinkish-peach color, a cosmetic attempt to hide all those Scotch-Irish freckles.

Puh-lease.

I didn't know at the time—and I would have laughed if you'd tried to tell me—that I'd just had my first glimpse of my future partner in the good life.

STEVIE'S POV

Let me interrupt here with some important information. While Sazan may have noticed my bad makeup job, let's just say the first thing I noticed about Sazan was what you might probably guess.

A pair of things. That come in twos. Epic, dramatic, right in your face.

That's right.

Her eyebrows. Seriously, our girl has incredible eyebrows. So when someone asks me what I first noticed about Sazan, I have to truthfully give all the credit to those flawless forehead parentheses.

Saz's eyebrows. They really are amazing.

Then I noticed some other things. But let's just leave it with the eyebrows, shall we?

What is a good life? We've all got our ideas about that. You've got yours. Advertisers have versions of the good life they're always selling us. Different cultures have their definitions, as do different faiths, and our parents have ideas of the good life they want for you and me.

So what is it? And how do we find it?

We (Stevie and Sazan) had many ideas of what we thought our good life would look like. We thought our good life would begin when we accomplished our goals, accumulated a certain amount in a bank account, and had the "right" people seeking us out to offer us bigger opportunities. That was the land we were heading for: the Land of the Good Life. But to get there, we thought we'd have to fight for it on the battleground. We'd push and drive. We'd sacrifice and keep sleep to a minimum. We'd hustle harder and aim bigger. We'd morph ourselves into whatever we needed to become to *earn* a good life from those who seemed to hold the keys to the doors we wanted to open. The good life was somewhere out there, if only we could just scramble and slash our way through every obstacle to reach it. And once we finally got there, to the good life, we planned to take a nap.

Only after years of pursuing the good life that way did we realize we were in danger of missing the real thing.

What about you? Have you dangled the good life out there in front of yourself, some days feeling like it was almost within reach, then finding it obscured by challenges and disappointments on other days? We understand. That's how it's been for us, too, through many seasons.

Chasing the good life also brings up weird competition vibes. When we don't feel we're living the good life yet—that we're still in pursuit of it—other people's seeming arrivals can make us feel flat. *We'll be living the good life,* we tell ourselves, *when we move into that house in the right neighborhood and deck it out perfectly in cottage-core.* Then a friend posts that she's just bought the house that looks so much like the one we're looking for. And she's somehow already managed to gut the thing and turn it into a Restoration Hardware look-alike model store.

And we're left feeling like we're missing out.

Maybe it's the cousin who gets engaged to the dreamiest guy. Or the best friend from college who lands the job we wanted. Or the door that closes, which we were convinced was the only portal available to the good life.

Where does that leave us?

We just keep putting off the good life, thinking it's not ours to have—at least not in our current situation.

Because of the way we used to look at the good life, and the way we used to think we had to frantically pursue it, we're passionate about sharing our journey. It's why we named our podcast *The Good Life.** It's why we talk about this topic all the time: because we know how we ran around in circles for it before we started to understand.

A good life is here for you. Right now. It's here. It's been yours. And it's also yours tomorrow. A good life is not about a time or a season. It's the continuum. A good life is built. Every day. It's there when you wake up in the morning. It's waiting for you in your turkey sandwich at lunch. It sits next to you in the afternoon meeting.

Finding your good life is simpler than you might think. A real good life is pieced together from the fabric of your days, from the bright blocks

---

* During my morning routine, I love to reflect on any habits I've fallen into that are keeping me from living my best life. So Stevie and I invited a brain coach onto the podcast to get tips on how to break the mold on those bad patterns. You can listen to that episode here: https://www.podcastone.com/episode/the-power-of-patterns.

of time you're given. It's stitched in place by what you do during those days, what you practice as your habits, what you say about your life, and the seasons you are living.

Because we believe in our bones that the good life is made of each moment, we've learned to think about living with intention through the phases of the day. In the morning, when we first get up and kick off the day, we each have some things we do that help us reflect on how we're going to spend our time and what our hearts need to look like. We have rhythms for midday, when we buckle down and work. We have priorities at evening—things we believe are important components of a good life. And then at nighttime we wind down, surrender to sleep, and rest. So strongly do we believe in the power of the phases of the day that we organized this book to follow that pattern, to keep you in the moment and help you recognize your good life as it's happening right in the moment.

As we've been talking and planning and working on this book, something has stuck with us. Think about the phrase "one day." It's a funny phrase because "one day" can refer to something from our past, such as, "One day, when I was a kid . . ."

But it can also mean something in the future, like when you say, "One day, I'm going to write that song."

Past and future all held in just a couple of short words: *one day*.

Here's something else that phrase has come to mean to us.

One. Day.

We have this *one day* in front of us. And what we do with this one day becomes an investment in a good life. This one day, *today*, can be a day in which we move closer to what we say is most important. This one day can be a day in which we act on the things we say are our highest values. There's a verse in the Bible that challenges us toward this in just a few words. It says, "Choose for yourselves this day whom you will serve" (Joshua 24:15). Because of our faith, we want to use our lives and our days to serve God's purpose. After all, we're serving *something* every day, right? It might be that we're serving some of our people-pleasing tendencies. It might be that we're serving some selfish ambitions. It might be that we are serving some fine obligations, but not the things we say are central to how we want to be spending our time.

Or we can spend this one day, the only one we currently have, thinking about one day long ago or fantasizing about one day to come. When we do that, we lose the gift of this one day. This one *real*, good day, no matter what it holds.

We've found that when we stay present in the part of the day we're currently living in, we stop racing ahead to the day after and the week after or staying stuck back in a time that has passed. We stay here, now.

> **What we do with this one day becomes an investment in a good life.**

And right now, fun, happy things are going on. And some tough things. Which is all good. The color and the fragrance make life beautiful. The textures of challenges and the hues of happiness.

It's significant that the Bible opens with God setting up time, setting up the way we humans experience a twenty-four-hour day. And we've been thinking about this: When God created the first day by placing the sun and the moon and the stars, then created the world his kids would live on, he wrapped up that project by calling it *good*.

This place in the universe where you live and we live, with its sunrises in the mornings and sunsets in the evenings? It was designed to be *good*.

Wherever you are right now, whatever your situation when you woke up this morning, you've received an invitation. You've been given this day, which will serve you a full dish of possibilities and emotions. You're going to laugh at moments. A couple of things might make you mad.

Three things will go according to schedule, and three things will run late or get canceled.

There's no need to wait for those things to happen before you can declare and believe deep down that you are living a good life. You just need to know how to see the good already in your days, then build toward that good. Gently. With kindness to yourself and others.

That's why we're so glad you're here. Because we believe in you, and we don't just want you to have the life you dream of. We want you to know that *you* are the dream, just as you are, now.

.   .   .

I saw Stevie again a few months later. We both started hanging out with fellow students who were part of the television degree program, which meant we found ourselves at a lot of the same parties and meetups. We also started working together more often at the television station, hosting news segments, creating promos, and doing voice-over work.

I told myself he wasn't my type. After all, he was white, and I didn't date white. He was the handsome, goofy, chatty, funny life of the party, and I had serious things to accomplish in my life. He was wildly charming, and I wasn't sure charming could be trusted. But life was good when Stevie was around. Very good. He made me laugh. He made our friends laugh. He was sentimental and kind.

He was . . . good.

Except our relationship wasn't all signed, sealed, and delivered. Breakups, breakouts, breakthroughs, and other events happened at breakneck speed along the way. There was joy and heartache, and times I thought it was all over. As deeply as we fell into friendship and romance and love with each other, we were each chasing our own ideas of a good life. And our ideas didn't always work together. At times we thought for each of us to have a good life, we'd have to live lives apart from each other.

Our understanding of living a good life needed some work.

It's taken a lot of living and a lot of mistakes and a lot of prayer and figuring things out. We've almost missed out on some good things while chasing after the notable, the celebrated, and the popular. We've had to learn truer definitions of what a real good life is and how it feels. We've had to stare down ambition and discontent and comparison because those things would love to convince us that what we thought was good, what we thought was enough, isn't.

Living the good life can be simple. Getting to the place where you believe that and lean into it often isn't.

Our first attempts at what we think could be an entry to the good life might be awkward. It might get interrupted. It might not feel like what we expected at first. You may have worked hard toward something you thought would pay off. You may have taken a risk that cost you. You might have headed one direction, only to realize it wasn't working. Whatever you've done, wherever you've been, whether you're feeling excited about building a good life or feeling a little road weary and jaded, I know something. I know it deep in my bones: your life matters.

Your life is unique and beautiful and carries its own story. But that doesn't mean you won't face challenges and trials. What it does mean is that you can live each day, whatever the day brings, knowing there are lessons and pleasures and peace and love and tenacity that are yours.

The environment you create in your home is part of your good life.

The routines you build into your day are part of your good life.

The friendships and romance you nurture are part of your good life.

The faith you build, the purpose of your life, and the growth you experience are part of your good life.

The way you treat yourself and what you say about yourself are part of your good life.

Your good life is in how you spend your mornings, your afternoons, your evenings, and your nighttime hours.

You are a good life. You love, and you try, and you get up again, and you learn. You might not see it just yet. You might not believe it just yet. But we're here, Stevie and I, to walk with you, share with you, cry with you, and laugh with you. The real good life is cherishing the simple things, slowing down, and creating moments for connection, joy, and love. We're honored to share our journey of learning to humbly recognize our good life. And we're here to celebrate yours.

MORNING

REFLECT

S omething is delivered to you, especially *for* you, right into your hands, every day. You first feel it when your mind rises from the lacy edges of your dreams and you remember. *This is my room. This is my bed. This is me.* At that first moment of waking, you receive it—one of the great mysteries of our existence.

It's a new beginning. Fresh and delivered to your door, bright and sweet, every morning. "Beginning" is one of the meanings of the word *morning*, a new start, a do-over, a clean page.

But something else can show up in the morning, hoping to stomp muddy footprints across that fresh page. The clanging alarm that goes off after too little sleep. Startling awake to the remembrance that you forgot to send that important email yesterday. Some of us wake up a little sunnier than others, and some of us have to wrestle our way to the surface.

And sometimes the voices in the morning prove the most difficult—the inner voice that tells you nothing can change. The thought that because yesterday was a mess, today will be too. The sneering echo that scoffs when you look for the good.

When we talk about living the good life, we have to start with good mornings. I (Sazan) love this quote from the novelist Daniel Handler. He wrote, "Morning is an important time of day, because how you spend your morning can often tell you what kind of day you are going to have."[1] For me, the morning is a time to reflect, meaning I start my morning by reflecting the good I want to see during the day. I think about how I want to live in the hours in front of me. And I want to mirror the truth that God is for me, and that he has good things in store.

That's not how I treated mornings for a long time. Mornings were something to be endured. Mornings were when I fought my way out of the sheets and into the slog of everything that needed to be done. Mornings kicked off a daylong siege of running after the things on my to-do list that I missed completing the day before. And then I would be surprised when the day continued in the same vein, the afternoon and evening hours feeling just as stressed and frantic.

But the years have taught me this much: How I build my mornings—how I choose to run my mornings instead of letting the mornings run me—makes a big difference in my ability to see and experience this good life. And I want to convince you of the same thing.

We will explore four truths about mornings together, you and I, over the next few chapters. It's a recipe I want to share. I love me a good recipe—the more tried-and-true, the better. You can tell the recipes I've pulled out time and again by the bent corners of the pages, the splashes of sauce, and the melted butter confetti on the paper. What I'm going to share with you is like that. These are the ingredients for a fantastic Good Morning; I hope you'll come back to them again and again. Just like any great recipe that becomes a favorite, you'll make your own tweaks and adjustments to it. You'll splash some of your own creation across these pages. And in so doing, you'll build approaches to your mornings that last throughout the day. It will take some work. It will take some experimenting. And it may also take changing your mind about some things, particularly if you don't consider yourself a morning person.

Right?

But stick with me. Because when you're building your beautiful and good life, mornings are your friend.

CHAPTER 1

REFLECT ON YOUR INTENTION

Teeny was really in her feelings.

Which meant I was too.

That girl. She's got my heart clutched firmly in her little five-year-old hands. Which means that when she's got a bad case of the feels, I've usually got one too. She's our firstborn, our Valentina Grace. She's big sister to Amari Rose, our three-year-old. And she's all things funny and feeling and passionate.

It had been a tough couple of weeks. Stevie and I were making adjustments to our work schedules. We had hired a new babysitter to come and help with the girls. We were feeling the pressure of a new product launch. And right in the middle of all that, Teeny had herself a little meltdown.

Except there's nothing teeny about a Teeny meltdown.

She offered up the whole nacho plate of emotions. She cried that she missed me. She wailed that she didn't want a nap time. She gave the new babysitter the frosty cold shoulder and refused to be entertained by the babysitter's best efforts. She began weeping during a conference call I was on. She needed more love, more attention, more affirmation than her usual serving. Which meant all the stuff that was supposed to be getting done was . . . not.

Those are the times as a mom when I then start questioning myself. *Am I being the best mom I can be to her? Is something else going on with her that I need to know about? Has another kid been mean to her? Am I messing everything up?*

And just like that, I could feel myself drifting into the oncoming traffic of self-doubt, condemnation, and a whole lot of other steely, mean edges.

But Stevie and I believe, believe big, that this is a good life we're living. And we believe it for you too. It's not easy to decide that you have a good life. You'll have days when it feels like anything but. All kinds of evidence to the contrary come flying your way sometimes, and it's hard to duck the sharp corners.

> **A good life doesn't just happen. You build it. Day by day.**

So it's important to have this truth fixed squarely on the dashboard of your life: A good life doesn't just happen. You build it. Day by day. It compounds interest, just like they teach you in your economics class in high school. Those days add up, and they equal a good life. The goodness has to be recognized. And you have to make room for it.

·   ·   ·

That night I collapsed into bed with Stevie, ruminating on yet another tough day with Teeny and her big emotions. I was already looking toward the morning with a sense of exhaustion. How was I going to wrangle Teeny and her feelings alongside everything I was supposed to get done the next day? My mind veered toward the garish, blinking sign of overwhelm I anticipated just a few hours ahead.

But then I remembered something.

Instead of grabbing our usual bowl of popcorn and binging our favorite show, I did something a little different. I started thinking about how to make the next morning the launching ground for a good day.

I decided to get intentional about the kind of morning I wanted us to have.

I used to think that *intention* meant "something I am sorta kinda planning to do or something I am hoping to make happen." Think about it: When we forget to send a thank-you note to a friend for a kind gift they gave us, we say, "I intended to send a thank-you, but . . ." Or we say we've been *intending* to get more serious about our health or that we *intend* to find a faith community that helps us grow and connect, but . . . *Intention* in the way we use it seems to be followed often by a *but*.

In reality, setting an intention is far more concrete than I originally thought. It actually means to turn your attention to something, to direct your attention to that thing. That's a lot more focused and far more purposeful than how we usually talk about intention. If I'm setting an intention for the day, it's much more than a wish for how I hope the day will go. It's more than a general sense of what would make for the kind of day I'd like to see.

Intention means choosing. I'm *deciding* what to pay attention to. I'm taking the finite budget of time I've been given for this day, and I'm sliding the coins that make up those moments across the table in the direction of good. Of peace. Of love. When it came to Teeny, I realized it wasn't enough to hope for a better day tomorrow. I needed to *create* the morning we needed to set the tone for the day.

Here's the thing. You're going to end up somewhere at the end of this day. You're moving toward something. You're steering there, whether you realize it or not. I'm all for letting a day unfold as it will, but when we make that our main way of navigating through life, we are more likely to veer closer to the frustrating, the dissatisfying, and the unfulfilling. Why does this happen? It's because of what I like to call *accidental intention*.

I know, I'm mixing two words that shouldn't be related. But that's the point. We often head where we don't intend. And it takes some course correction to move this one day in the right direction.

· · ·

Do you remember taking driver's ed? Which, by the way, let's take a moment to doff our fedoras in honor of those who get behind the wheels of real live cars to teach baby teenagers to head out on the road. It's an act of incredible bravery or masochism, but either way, #heroesamongus.

I barely passed driver's ed. Surely there's a special place in heaven for my driving instructor, because sixteen-year-old Sazan taking to the crazy Dallas highways and byways was a thrill ride for sure. Trying to stay focused on the road and the pedals and the steering wheel and the silent screams of my instructor was all a little much for me.

I blame part of my awkward driving skills on the fact that I never learned how to ride a bike as a kid. Think about it: Learning how to keep your balance and direct your handlebars in some kind of straight line seems like the intro course to later manning the wheel of a road machine. Alas, somehow, I made it to adulthood without any kind of biking experience.

When my fellow students in the UNT television department learned this little factoid about your girl Saz, that piece of hot goss spread like wildfire. "Sazan has never ridden a bike? Seriously! Is that even a thing? Isn't there some law that a kid has to know how to ride a bike before starting junior high?" All the smack talk resulted in a grand idea: a news segment featuring yours truly learning to ride a bike at the geriatric age of twenty-one. The piece was going to be creatively titled—wait for it— "Twenty-One-Year-Old Student Newscaster Learns to Ride a Bike."

Breaking news for sure. Maybe the syndicates would even want it. Or not.

Anyway, the day came when the cameras were fired up and a fellow class member by the name of Scott was to act as my biking teacher. Scott had entered the television degree program as a forty-year-old and was the proud dad of three little girls. He had successfully directed his girls from the non-biking camp to the biking group, and he felt confident he could teach me. Frankly, among all the other college-aged students in the department, Scott was the only one vaguely qualified for the task, as he was the only one of our classmates who had ever taught the art of biking.

My designated two-wheeler was rolled out. Now, here's an important detail. This was not some starter bike. No, it was a huge, manly bike. It was brown. It was dusty with grime on the wheels. It was tall. It was not Sazan-sized.

Scott was confident that we would conquer. I straddled that huge bike, sweaty palms on the peeling pleather handlebars, my right foot searching for the pedal, the toes of my left foot clinging desperately to the pavement through the sole of my shoe. "All right, Sazan," Scott crooned as the cameras rolled. "I want you to look straight ahead. Don't overthink it." I gave a slight push on the pedal with my right foot, and my left foot left the ground. "You got this!" Scott hollered as he gave the bike a shove.

Here's the thing about bike riding. People who do it make it look effortless. They glide across the pavement, they swerve in graceful loops, they speed up and slow down and spread their arms wide as they fly down the path. They make the bike look like an extension of themselves. They are the bike, and the bike is them.

The manly bike and I never enjoyed such a soul connection. Manly Bike was a mysterious behemoth, and I was a victim of a little thing people like to call *gravity.*

How hard can this be? I thought in the first five seconds of my bike ride. This thought was quickly followed by: *What in the world? How can I not do this?!* Which was then followed by a thought that was not in a known language but sounded a lot like panic.

The maiden voyage bike ride was over before it ever really started. I crashed into the grass next to the sidewalk. And I was done.

To be fair, I do think the manly bike was a big factor in this failed endeavor. Of course, there was one other detail I had failed to share with Scott the bike coach.

I have zero coordination. None. As in, at all. And amid my five seconds of biking glory and defeat, I wondered if coordination might also have something to do with conquering this skill.

But it wasn't just about my lack of coordination and the issues with Manly Bike. Scott's suggestion, to look straight ahead, seemed comical. How does one do that?! Trying to ride that bike felt like sensory overload. I was so aware of the cameras, trying to stay in the shot and keep my face at the right angle. I heard the cheers and gasps of my fellow students who lined the riding route. I sensed Scott and his hopes and expectations. The bike itself presented mechanics and brake levers and a dozen other things I wasn't sure how to operate. Not to mention gravity and balance and the uneven sidewalk. I had a million other things to focus on. Look straight ahead? *Exactly how am I supposed to do that,* Scott, *when there are a billion things going on?*

This is exactly what I mean by accidental intention. When I start off the day feeling like I'm teetering and tottering, my eyes go anywhere but ahead. I can get so distracted by the shiny objects on the side of the road of my life. I can be having a sweet day, then a text comes in with some challenging news about a business idea we have. Or I can get a mean DM from a stranger on the socials. Or *someone's* child throws a fit about being served milk out of the wrong cup (true story).

Before I know it, instead of steering toward peace and gratitude and joy, I'm veering onto the gritty shoulder of life, dirt spewing, feeling out of control. What's happened? Have the issues and rogue comments and temper tantrums shown up and thrown me off course? Is that what's going on?

Nope. Because those things are always going to show up.

It has to do with where I am intentionally turning my eyes.

I ran across this fancy phrase—"gaze strategy"—which refers to being intentional about where we look. Yes, it's a real thing. Yes, neuroscientists study it and write complicated research reports about it and disagree over certain nuances and develop all manner of theories. But at the end of the day, gaze strategy is about how we as humans are wired to move in the direction we're looking. When we head to a certain place, as we drive or walk or climb, we look to that end point, the goal we're aiming for. It plays out in our driving skills; when we take our eyes off the road to read that text that's come in, or we keep glancing at that new house's paint color, our gaze strategy isn't working for us. It's not helping us get to where we originally wanted to go safely.

I may intend for my day to be filled with flourishing moments and happiness, but when I take my eyes off that destination because of stress and ringing phones and other random distractions, I instead head straight for the things I *don't* want to make up the tenor of my day.

That's accidental intention. You don't mean for your day to go sideways. You don't wake up thinking, *Wow! I sure hope I get stressed about work and short-tempered with my kids and irritated at life in general today! What a vision!* No, we all want to have good days that build a good life.

But if you don't start your day with an *intentional* intention in mind, you'll probably end up with a bunch of accidental ones instead. That's why I want you to engage your gaze strategy. That's why I want you to start the day with a clear idea of where you want to go.

. . .

Back to the Teeny meltdown that wasn't teeny—to the night before, as I looked toward the coming morning with a sense of dread. It had been all too easy to keep my eyes on what had gone wrong that day. But God is good, and he has good days for us. And he especially has good ideas. I felt that quiet inner prompting to adjust my sight, to get a true gaze strategy mapped out, so I could better drive the day instead of letting the day drive me.

And that's why, the next morning, Teeny got up and discovered that her mom had mapped out the morning. Literally. I'd written up a little map of what we would be doing. We worked together to make her favorite pancakes. We spent some time reading her favorite books. We talked about her big feelings and her kind heart and her sweet dreams. We steered the morning instead of hanging on for dear life.

I'd love to tell you no meltdowns took place that day. I'd love to say that Teeny skipped and giggled through the rest of the morning and afternoon. That's not what happened. She still was especially needy for me, and she shed some more tears.

But I was back behind the wheel, moving through the miles, focusing on where I wanted to take us during the course of our day.

It was a good morning.

. . .

Let's build a gaze strategy for you. Your gaze strategy will help you stay in the lane of *intentional intention* (should I trademark that?) instead of accidental intention.

Here's how I set up my gaze strategy in this season of my life:

- I get up one hour earlier than the rest of my crew.
- I pull on workout clothes I've laid out the night before.
- I pad to the living room and light my favorite S+S Goods candle.*
- My golden retriever, Sweetie, is allowed to come with me, but that's because she knows how to lie back down and let me bask in the quiet.
- I get my favorite morning beverage and plant myself on our big, comfy sofa.
- I spend time in my favorite spiritual reading, which right now is the Psalms in the Bible. While I read, I watch the sun come up.

You might be thinking, *I'm not sure where the intention is in this scenario. Sounds like early morning reading on the couch.* And you wouldn't be wrong. But take a closer look.

- By getting up earlier than the rest of the family, I'm setting and fulfilling the intention of taking care of me, of making intentional time for myself.
- In pulling on my workout clothes, I'm being intentional about the next part of my morning, which is when I will work out. As part of my good life, I intend to take care of my body, and by pulling on my workout clothes, I've already made gains toward that intention.
- When I get to the living room and light that candle, I'm creating the atmosphere I want to be reflected in my home. I want our home to feel good and smell good and signal to everyone who comes to our home that it is a safe, loving place.

---

* Okay, shameless plug, but it really is what I do! You can restock or discover your favorite scent at the S+S Goods Shop here: https://stevieandsazan.com/collections/shop-s-s-goods.

- Sweetie as my quiet companion in the morning fulfills my intention to enjoy the quiet and to enjoy one of life's great and simple pleasures, a dog.
- That morning tea and snuggling into that sofa? The steps create a morning that I don't just think about or dream about or create only for a photo op on the 'gram. I am living how I present myself. I am making good on what I put out there. I intend to both create beauty in my work and be honest. And something as simple as taking to my couch with a yummy hot beverage fulfills that intention.
- When I pick up writing that feeds my soul, and I take some time in the morning to read wisdom and to build my faith, I'm not just hoping to live my life in step with God. I'm doing something about it.

My gaze strategy encompasses keeping promises to myself, taking care of myself, creating a home that speaks comfort and love, enjoying life's simple gifts, and living what I say I care about.

All before the rest of my people get up for the day.

Your gaze strategy is the secret to setting your intention. What are you steering toward?

I know an early morning habit like this can sound daunting, especially when you've got to get up super early for your commute to work, or you've got a new baby or puppy who's waking you up through the night. I've certainly had seasons, particularly during my fourth-trimester postpartum mode, when extra sleep was far more important than watching the sun come up. But don't miss this: That season had its *own* gaze strategy. It's not about the hour you get up. It's about *what* you do when you get up. It's about what you're doing when you get behind the wheel of your day.

It's about what you're looking at and the time you give yourself to make sure it aligns with where you want to go.

As you're learning to recognize and relish your good life, become a morning person. I'm not talking about getting up before the sun. I am talking about doing a self-check at the start of your day—whenever the day begins for you—to remember what is most important to you, to remember who you are and who you want to be, and to make sure the first moments of your day take you in that direction.

You'll begin to see your life as your *good* life when you look for the good and head that way, whatever the events of a day may bring. After all, as Ursula K. Le Guin wrote, "Morning comes whether you set the alarm or not."[1]

Sidenote: I intend to learn to ride a bike—as in, I've actually put it on a list of personal goals for this year. Stevie's family are all big bike riders, and they think

> **Your gaze strategy is the secret to setting your intention.**

because I can kill it on a stationary bike in the gym, it should be a no-brainer for me. But Stevie likes to remind me in a cycling class, where I'm smoking everyone in the room, "Little do these people know that you can't take this to the road." I'll need you to hold me accountable, dear reader. I intend to conquer the bike, but I've gotta intentionally intend to do it . . .

CHAPTER 2

REFLECT ON YOUR PACE

The alarm shrieked, my pulse jolted, and the day began. I (Sazan) wanted to hit the snooze alarm for an extra nine minutes of sleep, but I didn't dare. It was a Thursday morning.

I hated Thursday mornings.

Thursday Morning Hate started with Wednesday Night Angst. I would freak out before bed, trying to make sure I had all the things I needed for the next morning. I'd toss and turn through the night, checking my clock to make sure I hadn't overslept. And after a few hours of dozing, the alarm would blare while it was still pitch-dark outside, and it would be time to take on Thursday. Ugh.

I had to choose my concealer wisely because those bags under my eyes? They were poppin'. And not in a fresh, cute way.

Welcome to Los Angeles, my friend.

I'd left my family back in Dallas and was living the West Coast dream, newly married to Stevie and chasing spotlights and auditions. And it was paying off. Thursdays were my days to head to the *Access Hollywood* studios. There, I would do a live television segment promoting a variety of products.

I'd bought completely into the *livin'-the-life* hustle, grit, and grind gospel that was blasted from every corner of the internet and from every talent agent. Oh, and lest I forget, a big side helping of networking was also swirled into all that hustling and grinding. That formula for success was plastered all over the walls of my heart, just like my Blink-182 poster from back in the day. (Sidenote: During my Blink-182 phase, I really, really, really wanted to marry the lead singer, Tom DeLonge. It was a whole thing.) And here I was, living that life, trekking into literal Hollywood every Thursday to work on this well-known live show.

I was a stressed-out mess.

On Thursdays I'd shoot a couple of features, followed by a product modeling shoot and an influencer dinner that would keep me out until the wee hours. And when all that was done, I'd check my socials, make sure the next day's posts were ready to roll, chastise myself for the cheesecake I'd eaten at the influencer gathering, and then collapse into bed.

At some point, Stevie and I actually put together a video for our YouTube channel, a day-in-the-life kind of thing, that showed me up at the crack of dawn, running from studio to photo shoot to event to marketing meeting to influencer meetup. Everything was running me, instead of me running my life. I didn't realize at the time just how much control I had given up.

But this was what I'd been fighting for, right? I was on national television. I was going to the cool parties. I was in front of the camera and on the radar. So what was the problem?

Part of the Thursday Morning Hate was the actual work I was doing in front of the camera. I'd been hired to do these product-promotion segments—paid advertisements embedded into the show, presented as if *I* was selecting the items and talking about how much I loved them. And I have to say, sometimes it was for the dumbest stuff. Truly. It was like doing infomercials but live, trying to come up with anything redeeming to say about yet another antiaging foot cream. *Oh, look, a cream specially formulated for your feet! 'Cause normal lotion won't do for keeping your feet youthful!*

Eye roll.

And then there were those occasional weird things that would happen on set. Like the time a celebrity guest was going to be on the show. We passed each other in the hallway as I was rushing to my greenroom to figure out what to say to promote the latest-and-greatest antiaging foot cream on my segment. A few minutes later, an assistant knocked on my greenroom door.

"Um, Sazan," she said hesitantly. "Sorry to interrupt, but *so-and-so-sorta-famous-guest-who-will-not-be-named* sent me to ask if you'd like to join him in his greenroom?"

Excuse me? *So-and-so-sorta-famous-guest-who-will-not-be-named* is giving me a holler at this time of the morning? While I'm working? And has he seen Stevie Hendrix? You know, my H-U-S-B-A-N-D?

My reply was accommodating and gentle. *Not.*

"Tell *so-and-so-sorta-famous-guest-who-will-not-be-named* that I don't have time for that—that I'm working!"

Doing that gig for *Access Hollywood* wasn't a bad thing. I just didn't realize at the time that it wasn't feeding my soul. I was so busy—moving from one thing to the next so fast—that it didn't dawn on me to stop and ask myself: *Why?*

Why did I hate Thursdays, when, on paper, the opportunity looked like everything I'd been hustling for?

Why was fear coming over me on Wednesday nights?

The rat race had become my pace.

STEVIE'S POV

Listen, I'm not a jealous kind of a guy. But I've got to admit, when Saz came home and told me about the not-so-subtle "request" from *so-and-so-sorta-famous-guest-who-will-not-be-named*, your boy's inner Texan got a little riled. I was ready to head back to the studio and introduce *so-and-so-sorta-famous-guest-who-will-not-be-named* to a little Texas—ahem—hospitality. And understand, I know that Sazan, my spicy, devoted spitfire, is more than capable of putting anyone, celebrity or wannabe, back in their place. When Sazan says something is handled, it's handled. But it was definitely a moment when I wanted to go all Alamo on Mr. California and tell him "not cool."

It would be a lot cleaner if I could say that hustling and grinding and all the rest doesn't work. It would be a lot neater to tell you that living "the life" is all the fuel you need.

Here's the thing about that combo: It can work. It *does* work, a lot of the time.

Was I living the life? Absolutely. Was it exciting and fun and sometimes glamorous? Yep.

Was I also wildly overwhelmed and exhausted and feeling out of control?

Also yes.

I get how that could sound ungrateful or trite. But somehow, someone else had started beating the drum that signaled the pace I ran every day, and that cadence kept speeding up.

It makes me think about the graph that's created when you wear a heart monitor. It spikes up and drops down. There's the beat of your heart and the rest that follows. Everyone has their own specific rhythm to their beating heart. Some people's hearts run a little faster and some a little slower. Our lives are like that too. High moments that feel great. Low moments that feel uncertain or scary. The image is of a pace that's unique to me and unique to you. As a matter of fact, your EKG is so specific to you, some technologies out there are exploring how to use it for identification purposes, just like a fingerprint.[1] And yet, here we all are, trying to keep pace, keep the beat with each other.

I recently saw the movie *Elvis*, the Baz Luhrmann creative biopic of the King of Rock and Roll, Elvis Presley. I was struck by how Elvis experienced phenomenal success, but the pace required for what he was doing was simply beyond what a healthy human being could do. And so, the solution for keeping the beat was a wild blend of drugs from his doctors, which led to a dependence that would ultimately be his undoing. And it happened because he lost the ability to set his own pace amid his search for achievement and fulfillment.

The good life has a rhythm. And rhythm has a lot to do with agreement between the elements of an orchestra. It has a lot to do with how proportionate the tempo is.

I love watching drum majors at football games—the confidence with which they pump those batons up and down. (Which, for a bonus trivia round, is called a drum major mace. You're welcome.) You've got all these people out on the field, all with different notes to play and steps to take, but the drum major gets everyone at the same pace, sets the beat for the music, and keeps everyone marching in time. Which is great. Unless you're building a good life and want to march to the beat of your own drum. In that case, having to look to a drum major in the forms of people's opinions or expectations or our own interpretation of what we think it will take to achieve what we want becomes the beat we feel compelled to march to.

That's not to say that you can't experience the good life if someone else—such as your boss or your newborn—is calling the shots for a while. What it does mean is that when you are living your good life, you have to stay aware of the pace at which you're living. And make some adjustments as needed.

So why do we so often turn over the drum major position to our employer or our volunteer projects or our extended family or the expectations of our community?

There's something I've been learning. It's taken me awhile because it seems counterintuitive to what we're often taught about achieving the good life. And that's the power of going slow.

To grow, go slow.

> **Stay aware of the pace at which you're living.**

I know, that sentiment probably doesn't match up with what the *Grow Your Online Business at the Speed of Light* digital course had to say. You've probably had full helpings, just like I have, of getting up earlier than everyone else; hitting the day with a heavy dose of brutal, gasping cardio; using the planner that plots out every second of every day; and getting your inbox to zero before you hit the pillow at night.

Is discipline a component of the good life? No doubt. But did you ever think about this? It takes discipline to go slow.

I love to work out. But I can remember times—in the name of being efficient and in light of a packed schedule—I would hit the gym and lift weights like I was on helium. I could whip through a lifting list like nobody's business. But guess what? Trainers tell us that the best growth comes when we slow down—when we make our muscles work the full scope of lifting that weight, then *control, control, control* putting down that weight. That's when the real growth begins. That kind of work takes a level of discipline that our culture doesn't always value.

The discipline to take your time. The discipline to choose a different pace than the rest of those in the race.

Does setting a different pace for your life make you lazy? Not at all.

Sleep is an experience that feels like it exists outside of time. When I'm sleeping, when I'm deep in my dreams, time morphs and expands and contracts without a care given to the clock. But the minute I open my eyes in the morning, well . . . That right there tells the story, doesn't it? *The minute I open my eyes.* Time comes back online, and the beat of my day, the percussion soundtrack, starts moving along at a staccato.

Yes, I've left behind the frantic clip of my Los Angeles days. But I've learned that, no matter the conditions of my season of life, I can all too easily relinquish control of the clock to other people's expectations and preferences. At times I've allowed my days to become just as harried while caring for two toddlers at home as I did when running between television studios out in California.

Why does that happen?

Each of our lives has a pace. Yes, time is recorded by the clock. But the way we experience that time, the way we move through those moments? That's up to us. Have we created some margin for ourselves? Or have we scheduled everything down to the second? Have we allowed a cushion for when the computer needs a reboot, for when the toddler has a meltdown, for when our partner needs our listening ear just a little longer? Or have we become so task- and meeting- and appointment-oriented that any tack in the road puts us at risk for a total blowout?

Look, I know that having someone alongside you who helps set the pace for a run can be helpful. You might find you can go longer than you would have on your own. You might find yourself running the miles a little faster than you would have on your own. But what is your goal? Do you need to run longer? Do you need to run faster?

That's what I had to ask myself about the pace of my life while I was out in LA. Who was I trying to keep up with? Why? And who in my life seemed unhappy with my pace? Were they people who deserved that level of influence in my life? Or had I simply accepted the pace at which everyone around me seemed to be running?

I continue to ask myself those questions even now, when the momming gets crazy and the schedule gets too full.

I learned something else about myself and pace. Sure, there are those people in my world and in yours who seem to thrive by going full tilt all the time. They seem energized, happy, and focused. Me?

That speed wore me out. Instead of feeling a regenerating excitement, I found that the pace of life was depleting my joy.

What does all this have to do with your morning?

Morning is the time of day that often sets the pace. Just like we talked about with intention, if we're not aware of the pace we're setting, it's all too easy for us to get pulled into the current of appointments and phone calls, grocery store runs and playdates, without stopping to ask ourselves and important question: *Why?*

Maybe you feel like you have very little control over the pace of this season of your life. Maybe you're working for a boss who is always moving at full throttle and expects you to do the same. Maybe you're working a full-time job but you're also building your side hustle, and it's keeping you running from dawn 'til midnight. I get it. But what I want you to think about is this: Do you have to do *all* the things? Are there some things you can let go of right now?

Let's say you are building your career, you've got a young child, and you're married. Now I just bet people in your world are often asking you to do more. There's the nice lady at church who wants you to volunteer in children's church. There's your friend who really, really wants you to sign up for a Pilates class with her twice a week. There's a book club or a hobby or a community initiative, and you feel like everyone else is doing it.

Friend, before you go putting your name on all those rosters, I want you to hit pause. Think about it.

Is this really the season to sign up for one more thing? Or would your heart and home and nerves do a whole lot better if you slowed down a little?

The more I "go with the slow," the more I believe it and see the wisdom of it. I'm not making decisions from a frantic place. I'm not running on nervous, caffeine-fueled stress, but from a thoughtful, considered mindset. And I'm convinced that pace has everything to do with living a good life. Going at breakneck speed may be exhilarating for a while, but it will catch up with you. Your body will start talking to you, and you won't like what it's saying. Your mind

> **Do you have to do *all* the things?**

will keep racing long after you've put your tired bones to bed. You'll make impulsive decisions because you're trying to move *fast, fast, fast*, and some of those decisions will not be the ones you would've made had you taken a little more time to think.

Have you ever thought about what you miss by going fast?

In the early days of my career, I allowed myself to be pulled into the pace of the influencers and brand ambassadors around me—at least, what I *thought* their pace was. A brand would contact Stevie and me to make a video, by tomorrow if possible, with all kinds of specs and details. And Stevie and I would jump on it, no matter what we had planned that day, no matter the kind of time a project like that would take. We'd cancel plans with friends, guzzle some more coffee, break out the camera equipment, careen to optimal spots for shoots, and capture the video and images—all while watching the clock and the waning sunlight. Then we'd go screaming back to the house for an all-night editing session. We did stuff like that over and over.

But the more we learned about pace and the more we realized we had allowed the drum major of expectation to run us in circles on the field, the more we leaned into the slow. We had to unlearn some muscle memory, the kind that keeps you answering the phone or responding to the text or replying to the email after you promised yourself it was time to shut it down for the rest of the night. We had to overcome the worry that we'd miss out on some amazing opportunity if we didn't obey the pace set by a brand or last-minute marketing push.

Committing to your own pace takes courage. It takes commitment. Because it will be challenged. I can promise you that.

STEVIE'S POV

I see the issue of pace as one of extremes. Some people are constantly teetering on the edge of burnout. Then I know some people who can't get off the couch.

Both situations are problematic. Go too fast and you'll flame out. But if you're unwilling to push yourself, you might find that the only kind of impression you're making in your life is in the couch cushions. Whether over-fast or over-slow, people seem to have a natural bent for one setting or the other.

That's why you need to evaluate your tendencies.

Do you take on too much? Or do you tend to pull back from challenging projects or adventures?

When you're honest about your tendencies, you can devise a better strategy for staying at a pace that is healthiest for you.

Saz and I, we're both Team Burnout. And once we admitted that to ourselves, it allowed us to better monitor what we are doing and how close to the line we are living. We have established that our relationship with each other and our relationship with our kids are the two top priorities in our home. And when we keep them at the top, it helps us evaluate what should be a yes and what should be a no. It's tricky, because sometimes priorities can feel a little selfish. There are things we *could* do. We *could* make an exception—bounce date night to the next week, squeeze in one more meeting, and then try to make it up to the kids over the weekend.

But that's not the pace we want to model for our family. And it's not the pace that honors what we say is most important.

Here's the flip side. If you tend toward Team Couch, then it might be time to pick up the pace a bit. If you want to experience certain things as part of your good life, then you may have to get a little uncomfortable first. This idea makes me think about what fitness experts say a good running pace is: If you can't talk while running, you're going too hard for the long haul. But if you're not even slightly out of breath, then you're not growing in endurance. You're not building fitness.

A good life is a fruitful life. So what are you producing with your pace?

If the fruit is more and more stress, slow down. If the fruit is procrastination, sidestepped goals, and relying on others to take care of your needs, it's time to increase your stride and cover some ground. I love this verse when I think about the ideal pace of life: "Let us run with perseverance the race marked out for us" (Hebrews 12:1). A specific race is marked out for me. And a specific race is marked out for you. Our job is to each run our race and to persevere. Perseverance is when we take on our lives in a sustainable way that provides just enough challenge to help us grow stronger.

I'm seeing now what I would have missed if I had stayed on the treadmill of busy. And the better pace of life is coming off the treadmill and learning to stroll. To walk while taking in the details of your life, instead of letting your life flicker by while you're chasing everyone else. Here's some good news. You don't have to sprint to keep up with the pack. You don't have to slow down if you're having a good run. You get to choose your pace of life—and you can run that pace instead of letting it run you.

How do Stevie and I do this?

At the end of each year, we take a look at how we paced our lives for the previous 364 days. We evaluate the year and talk about how it felt. Did it feel like we made room for the experiences, adventures, goals, and rest that we intended at the beginning of the year? Did we hit our date nights each week like we said we would?

Sometimes during that evaluation, we realize that while we did a lot of cool stuff, we still aren't feeling as connected. Take note of this important caution light: Is all that stuff you're doing taking you where you want to go, directing you to what's most important to you? We're learning that if connection with each other is the primary goal, then we need to identify the moments and seasons that made us feel the most connected.

Don't feel like you have to wait until the end of the year to do your own evaluation. Start today. What is most important to you in your good life? Write it down. Then take a look at the activities and the to-dos that are filling your day. Are they putting you on the right track for what you say you want in your life? Sometimes we need to give ourselves permission to get off the track we're on and explore other ways to live.

Maybe you have a work situation that is keeping you running day and night. What's behind that? Could you cut some expenses to allow you to exit that track? Are you on that track because of someone else's expectations? Get honest with yourself about why you're running at the pace you are and just who you might be running for. There are different kinds of paths paving the way to the places you're looking for. Sometimes you're on the highway, flying fast. Other times, you need to be on the service road, avoiding the chaos of the speedsters. The scenic route is often a better way to go. Just because you pulled onto a certain kind of path doesn't mean you have to stay there.

Rest is a risk. A reasonable pace is a redeeming perspective. When the pace is right, you can *see* your life as you live it, instead of the days becoming a blur as you speed past.

So pick a good pace—one that matches your season of life, one that lets you rest and play and work in equal measures. Just like your heartbeat, you were created with a unique rhythm. And it's a good one.

CHAPTER 3

REFLECT ON YOUR WORTH

Post-Nap Toddler Breath is my *favorite favorite favorite* scent in the whole world. I (Sazan) am the weirdo who grabs Amari just after she wakes up, then I shove my nostrils near her rosebud mouth to breathe her in, deep into my lungs. She's earthy and sweet and a little sour and something uniquely her own. But you probably can't make a candle out of that.

I mean, you could, but it would be a tough one to market. And what kind of logo would you put on that kind of a thing?

Coming in a close second—particularly if we're talking scents you can actually bottle or turn into candles—is a combination of fall aromas: vanilla, tobacco, amber, and Fraser fir. Those scents are cozy and soothing, clean and sweet. For me, lighting a candle is a go-to step for making our house feel like home.

It had long been a dream of ours to develop a line of home goods, including candles, that would be high-quality, timeless, good-smelling, and great-looking in your home. The process for designing and putting together collections of items has been a learning curve. It's been fun and rewarding to see people sharing how they're using their finds from the S+S Goods Shop.

Something you have to figure out early on in the product business is how to price the things you're selling. Pricing seems like it wouldn't be all that hard; after all, similar items out there are already being offered by other businesses, and they've all made decisions about what price tags to put on their items. But it took us awhile to wrap our heads around what our goods were worth.

First you have the actual cost of the materials needed to produce the item. Next, the behind-the-scenes research costs: the hours put into analyzing customer demographics and what scents and textures people like. Don't forget the cost of developing and running the website where you'll fulfill orders and market your products.

There is also that murky world of trying to understand what people are willing to pay for something. You may come up with the greatest widget or gadget in the world, made with all the best ingredients and heart and effort and quality. But if the price tag on it is too high, you could miss out on customers who would love what you're selling but can't afford it. On the other hand, if you set the price too low, people could perceive it as being lower quality.

I can promise you, those S+S Goods meetings—the ones where we talk about all things pricing—can make your head pound. And then spin.

One more component of pricing strategy is a little more meta. And that is, what do we think a product is *worth*? Beyond the necessary ingredients, customer research, social stats, and the competitors' products, what value do we believe this product has in our own lives and in our home?

These discussions had me thinking a lot about how I determine the worth of a lot of things in my life. Is a new opportunity *worth* chasing when it could cost me some peace? Is the thing Stevie's doing that's annoying me worth a fight? Is that latest movie that's available to stream worth missing some sleep? (And you know your girl loves her sleep.)

This whole notion of worth has been haunting me for a lot of my life: What is my worth? How do I determine it? Is it based on the business I build? The television contracts I get? The kudos I receive when I'm in the spotlight?

Am I worthy on this one day, or am I striving to be worthy enough one day?

·   ·   ·

Stevie and I were excitedly preparing to launch our debut candle and introduce it into our S+S Goods line. One of our friends, an extremely talented graphic designer, had put together the most gorgeous branding. We named the candle Cottage in the Woods with the subtext "Goodness Is All Around." This was the entire message behind the campaign and brand launch. The scent was everything I wanted it to be, and the packaging was fantastic. It had been a long process, with tons of meetings about what the label should look like. After all, this was the flagship product of our new line, and it had to be polished and perfect.

We'd gone over the graphics multiple times with our small mom-and-pop team, and everyone was so thrilled with the final version. We sourced all the best ingredients. We found the perfect manufacturer. Everything went into production. Stevie and I could not wait for this candle to go out into the world.

We were on a big family trip to Colorado the week the candle became available in our shop, appropriately staying in the coziest cottage in the Breckenridge woods (#onbrand). Us being us, we talked about it on our social media channels. We did all the things you're supposed to do: Dreamy posts with gorgeous pictures of the candle. Stories where we talked about the process of creating the candle. Videos on what it takes to bring a product you've created to the market. All. The. Hashtags. People started buying the candle and were loving it. Within two days, our first candle was officially sold out.

Ah. The thrill of a successful product launch. The happiness of making people happy.

And then . . .

A sweet follower sent us a DM on Instagram. It was so kind.

"Hey, you guys," she wrote. "So excited for you about the new candle. But, um, did you notice there's a typo on the label?"

WHAT?!

That couldn't be right.

I'd looked at that label approximately six billion times! We all did! I frantically bailed out of my DMs and went over to my posts. I scanned down my feed to the gorgeous photo of our beloved Goodness Is All Around candle. I breathed a sigh of relief. It was fine.

Wait . . .

No no no no no.

It couldn't be.

Instead of "Goodness Is All Around," the flowing calligraphy said "Goodness Is All Aound."

AOUND?

A-O-U-N-D.

Dude.

I started to spin like *Wheel of Fortune*. *Pat, can I pleeeeaaase buy a consonant instead of a vowel? Just one little* r? *Please?!?*

I scrunched my eyes shut in the desperate hope that the next time I opened them and looked at the candle post, the *r* would magically appear.

No such luck.

No matter how many times I blinked, no matter how hard, goodness was still all AOUND.

·   ·   ·

I get lots of comments and questions from my online community and from people who come across our content. And I've got to say, embedded in some of those comments and questions, I can hear a pulse that makes me a little sad.

Sometimes I can hear it in critical comments, or the negative feedback of someone questioning why we think we should be posting. Sometimes I hear it in a sweet DM, like, "I just love following your life. I could never have anything like that."

I can hear this particular pulse because a similar one beats in my own soul at times. It's the unsettled question about worth.

That person who is picking apart my life and Stevie's? I have a lot of compassion for them because I know that someone who is happy in their own life doesn't have time to pull apart someone else's. Someone who knows their own worth isn't looking to minimize anyone else's.

And in those sweet comments, when someone claims they can't have a life they love, I hear it there too.

Am I worthy?

What is my worth?

I'm telling you: You need to settle this question at the top of every day, in the early hours of the morning.

> **Someone who knows their own worth isn't looking to minimize anyone else's.**

I am not worthy because of what I accomplish during the upcoming day. I am not worthy because of what my bank account holds or doesn't hold. I'm not worthy because of my personal history or current circumstance.

I'm worthy because the Creator of the universe says I am. God has already adjourned the team meeting about all the ingredients that make me *me*, and he's decided I'm valuable. Precious. Irreplaceable. Unique.

And so are you. Your worth has already been settled. And you need to check in on that truth every morning.

STEVIE'S POV

I do something with the girls every morning, and I really believe it makes a difference. We say together, "Today is going to be a great day!" We say it big and we say it with a lot of enthusiasm. We're not going to just have a day; we're going to have a *great* one.

What does that have to do with your worth, you might ask? This.

The words line us up with what God says about us. He sent Jesus to be our friend, to give us great days. He walks beside us every day as a friend. Even on the days we don't feel like we're enough. Even on the days we want to pick ourselves apart. And if we are worthy enough for friendship with God, then why not call it a great day?

When I remind myself that it's going to be a great day, I'm reminding myself that I'm showing up, that I'm needed, and that I have choices to make. I'm choosing the option that lines up with what I believe God wants for me and for you—to live beautiful, powerful, memorable moments.

Try it. Call your day a great day first thing in the morning, and see if it helps settle your worth. Remembering your worthiness to live this day well may encourage you, like it does me.

The reason I want you to be intentional in the morning hours about settling your worth is that it will drive so many of your interactions with yourself and others throughout the day. If you don't have a settled "price" for your time, you'll allow others to pull you into their priorities instead of accomplishing yours. If you haven't gotten clear about your worth, you'll spend a lot of time trying to prove it. And if you're looking to others to tell you what your value is, if you're grabbing your phone, scrolling through the valley of the shadow of Instagram each morning, or if you're waiting for someone to encourage you or compliment you or validate the direction you're heading—then you and your understanding of your worth are at the mercy of another person or thing. You're attaching your understanding of your value to their opinion. Someone else's opinion of you should never be how you determine the price tag of your life.

And then there's this.

I firmly believe that if you have not settled your own worth, if you are still wrestling with valuing and loving yourself fully, you won't be able to extend that same kind of love and appreciation to the people in your life. Hard stop.

Think about it.

If you're a mama raising babies, but you're not sure about your value, or if you've attached it to how clean the house is or how fancy the dinners you make are, then you're going to model that kind of worthiness system to your kids. You may tell them often they are awesome for who they are, but if they don't see you living by that standard, they'll believe your actions over your words.

If you're single and you're attaching your worth to the romance you have in your life, you'll give off the vibe that you're not worthy just as you are. Your worth doesn't change when a man comes into your life or when he leaves.

Maybe you've been attaching your worth to how well your side hustle is going or the grade you're earning in that tough class toward your degree. Maybe you've determined your worth by how proud your parents are of you.

Look, your girl Saz is all about doing her best. I'm all about giving things my all. But you're still worthy on the days when you're just having to push through. You're still worthy after the breakup. You're still worthy when the world says you don't measure up. You're still worthy after the award, and you're just as worthy when the score doesn't go your way. I wish someone had told me this ten years ago, particularly on a day when I was heartbroken and crying on my bedroom floor, questioning everything in my life, wondering if it was worth living. I had that rock-bottom moment when my sense of my value was so low, it was costing me every bit of peace, every sliver of joy.

Walking in the assurance of our worth makes us better people.

Not feeling worthy can make us competitive in all the wrong ways.

We feel we have to scramble to get the attention of that cute guy in our class who has the eye of all the other girls. We feel we have to earn better grades or perform better athletically to get our parents' approval amid a houseful of siblings. We evaluate our social media platforms based on how many likes our posts receive versus other accounts.

Worth and competition always seem to be locked in a vicious waltz, stepping on each other's toes, each one trying to lead.

When I began my faith journey as I entered adulthood, my perceived value to the world, of the worth I would have, was tied to all kinds of factors. What would my parents think about certain aspects of my life? What did I need to do to prove my worth to potential brands and platform investors? How could I make a producer see what I could bring to the table? I saw the world through this kind of lens: *The value I bring to others and to the marketplace will determine my worth.*

So you can imagine my confusion—and frankly, my level of pushback—when I began to encounter a God who told me I had worth that was not attached to any of those things, but that I was a dearly loved child simply because I existed.

You'd think this would be good news to me, but it took a long time for this truth to settle in my soul. It's funny, the things we fight back against are often the things that could bring us so much freedom. But we've been steeped so long in a different tea of definition that we've become stained by it. To receive that I was loved—the end, period—meant no longer looking at my life and my value through my résumé. But it also meant my worth would no longer be determined by my effort. And my effort was where I still felt a sense of control.

That's the thing about learning to believe we are loved and valued beyond what we can do and earn. It means letting go of a system that keeps people on different rungs of the ladder. It means letting go of evaluating others by what they can do for us and what they've achieved. And it means we have to stop looking at ourselves that way too.

Have you ever diminished yourself in a meeting because you didn't want to make anyone mad? Or have you put up with a guy who is always late to pick you up for a date? Or who "forgets" to call you back over and over?

Friend, you're underestimating your worth.

Part of my problem was that I was looking at my own worth through a classic economic lens. Maybe you remember this from an economics course in school: typically, the price of something is set where supply and demand meet. If you're in the job market, and a whole lot of other people have the same degree or skill set, that's the supply. And if only a handful of companies are currently hiring for positions requiring your degree or skill set, that would be an example of demand. In such a scenario, a lot of people will be competing for the same job, and the employer will likely be able to set the "price" they're willing to pay—the salary for your time—at a lower rate.

For me, I knew lots and lots of people wanted to get into careers in television. At every audition, at every casting call, loads of people vied for just a handful of spots. It messed even further with my understanding of my worth, this economic way of looking at myself. In my head, it went something like: *There are jillions of girls like me, all wanting the big break, all hoping to exude the "it factor." I've got to be extra special and hardworking and intense and driven to even compete with so many people.*

You can't change the realities of the work marketplace. You can't change the economic factors in play when it comes to compensation and opportunity.

You *can* decide that *your* worth will not be attached to these things. And you can flip that idea of worth on its head, looking instead at all the things pulling you in different directions:

Is it worth your time?
Is it worth your attention?
Is it worth your peace?

·   ·   ·

Back to the label fiasco.

I can't begin to tell you how frustrated I was. We'd spent all this time getting every detail just right. Now we had this glaring mistake on this premium candle.

Talk about embarrassing.

40

Sure, my first thought was how mad I was at the designer. How could she have let this slip through? Then I was mad at myself. How had I missed it, over and over?

Then a certain truth came shining through.

See, even though the label wasn't right, the ingredients were. No matter what the label said, the beautiful scent was worth the price. While we wanted the packaging to be gorgeous, of course, it was really about what went into the candle itself that determined its value.

Now, won't that preach?

One of Stevie's favorite stories in the Bible is about a woman who meets Jesus at the well in her town. She's got a pretty sketch reputation. She's been with a lot of guys, and you can bet in her small town that everyone knows her reputation. But Jesus treats her with compassion and respect. He lets her know she has the same access to God and to eternal life as anyone else, regardless of her past, through him. He says, "Whoever drinks the water I give them will never thirst. Indeed, the water I give them will become in them a spring of water welling up to eternal life" (John 4:14). Stevie loves to call this story "Well of Worth" because Jesus reminds someone who is considered less-than by her culture that she is worthy and treasured in the eyes of God.

I'm not going to get my presentation right every time. I'm going to have days when my best doesn't feel top-shelf. But that's not what my value is about.

My worth is found in the inner stuff—what I'm made of, created of. The fact that God calls me worthy. Just like he does for you.

My mistakes don't affect my worth. Your mistakes don't affect yours. And when I can begin the day giving myself the grace of that truth, it's going to be a good day.

Stevie and I could have gone on a hunt to take names and assign blame with the AOUND fiasco. But really, what would that have accomplished? The whole thing felt like God's way of humbling us.

We'd been so focused on making everything perfect, so buttoned-up and proper. And here we were, learning the lesson again that perfection can't be the goal.

I've made plenty of mistakes. You have too. Those mistakes are just that: mistakes. They're not deductions of the value of who you are.

Here's the hilarious legacy from that label debacle. "Goodness is all aound" has become something of a family motto. Stevie and I quote it all the time to each other. It's the spot-on reminder that goodness does surround us, even when we get the label wrong, even when we blow it in spite of our best efforts.

How about this?

WOTHY.

W-o-t-h-y.

You are w-o-t-h-y of goodness in your life.

You're worthy, even when you skip the *r*. You're worthy, even when it doesn't feel like it. And when you begin your day reminding yourself of this fact, you're giving yourself permission to notice what is beautiful. You're building a day in which you have nothing to prove and everything to appreciate.

> You're building a day in which you have nothing to prove and everything to appreciate.

When I settle my worth, first thing in the morning, I begin my day in freedom.

So say it with me.

"I am w-o-t-h-y."

And:

"Goodness is all a-o-u-n-d."

CHAPTER 4

REFLECT ON WHAT YOU SAY TO YOURSELF

Yes, mornings are for reflection. For setting the pace. For settling your worth.

But mornings are also about Teeny's hair.

In my opinion, doing your five-year-old's hair can qualify as your meditation. It's one of the most therapeutic things in my day. I get the girls up and get them ready for their day. And a chunk of that time is for brushing out the tiny little knots that have come to nest in Teeny's hair during her night's sleep.

Teeny's hair basically goes to war with her pillow during the night. When she gets up in the morning, her hair is a mass of mayhem. When

I get hold of her with the hairbrush, transforming her sable brown tresses back to their sleek beauty and softness brings me a sense of calm.

When she was about three and a half, she began reminding me a lot of myself at the same age. My mom tells stories of when I was a child— that even at a really young age, I was hyperfocused on my hairstyles. I reportedly was also very particular in my choices of fashion and clothing. Yep, even as a preschooler, your girl was bringing the style. And Teeny seems to have inherited that.

What I remember is being pretty clear as a kid about how I wanted to present myself.

I had a special toothbrush that was specifically for wetting and brushing my bangs. Yes, I had a bangs toothbrush. (Product opportunity? I should run this by Stevie for the S+S Goods Shop . . . JK.) And styling those bangs was a whole thing. I wanted my bangs completely wet. I wanted them flat against my forehead, with no gaps. I had a name for what all this effort was helping me avoid: split bangs. Split bangs were a no-go. No sliver of my forehead was allowed to show. Any peek of the territory above my eyes was absolutely unacceptable. The hair also had to be stick straight. I had bangs rules, and they had to be followed to the follicle.

This whole process was a serious time commitment. My mom cut my bangs for me and, no offense to my mom, there were a lot of uneven bangs to be tamed. We're not talking about bangs with some kind of texturing. This was a solid curtain of naturally curly hair, chopped off at the eyebrows. What happens to naturally curly hair when you take off the length? You got it. Frizz City. It took real dedication to my art to get those bangs slicked down and in place.

After accomplishing that part of my morning beauty routine, I would then move on to brushing out my hair. I'd brush and brush and brush. As a kid, this seemed to take hours. It was the barometer of my day, how those bangs turned out and how my hair looked.

While my mom was allowed to cut my bangs, she was not allowed to style my hair. How she had the patience to stand by while I combed through strands of hair with a toothbrush, I'll never know.

I even used to make up excuses while we were in public to go find a mirror and check on my coiffure. "Mommy," I'd say while visiting friends in their home, "I need to go to the bathroom. I really, really need to go." Nothing sets a mom on a mission like a preschooler doing the potty dance. She'd take me to the restroom, and I'd immediately park myself in front of the mirror for a bangs check. It would calm me down. I'd make a few adjustments, back to perfect. My mom would catch my eyes in the mirror and say, "Did you just tell me you needed to go to the bathroom *so you could check your hair?*"

You should see the pictures of me as a kid, rocking all these crazy hairstyles I created every morning. Yeah, you *should* see them. But you won't. I've got those bad boys under lock and key because I figure the public got enough of an eyeful every time I went out as a kid. Truly, these hairstyles I labored over were bananas.

And I love that my mom just let me do it.

She gave me the creative freedom to go into the bathroom and get into her bobby pins, scrunchies, and hair ties. Mom basically let me raid all her stuff, including toothbrushes (ahem), and let me create.

So my "look" development was going on. But I would also talk to myself in the mirror. As I was adjusting and pinning and scrunching, I'd talk myself through it. Except it wasn't myself, at least in my head. It was a character I named Castanada.

Why Castanada, you ask? I have no idea. But that was her name, the girl I talked to in the mirror. Castanada.

I'd explain to Castanada why we were going for a side pony with a couple of pieces of hair pulled loose in front of my ear. I'd update Castanada on the best methods for plastering bangs to my forehead. Castanada would smile encouragingly at me. I was really helping Castanada with these premium content tutorials.

My family lived in a tiny two-and-a-half-bedroom apartment. I say two-and-a-half-bedroom because my parents put an extra twin bed in the small laundry room, and that became another spot for a kid. We had one and a half bathrooms, so you can imagine the traffic jam I created hogging the bathroom mirror and holding these conversations with Castanada. As a result, anyone who came into the bathroom while I was there became part of the narrative.

My sister would wander in, and she'd be introduced into the conversation. And her girl in the mirror was named Jelly. Now there were even more people to show off different techniques to. When another family member would enter the bathroom chat and try to shoo us out, that character in the mirror became Mr. Jelly. (It was unclear if Mr. Jelly and my sister's friend Jelly were related or not. I'm just reporting the facts here.) He was very aggressive in trying to kick my sister and Jelly and Castanada and me out of the bathroom. Mr. Jelly was a real pain because he just couldn't seem to understand the artistic process.

Growing up, my siblings and I didn't go to sleepover parties or anything like that. But I didn't mind. I had this amazing imaginary friend in Castanada and a whole cast of characters who were so real to me.

Here's what I recognize now about my mom's genius approach. She was letting me explore and try new things. She had no way of knowing it at the time, but when she left space for me to make up new looks and express myself, she was preparing me for what would become my career. Think about it: no social platforms existed back in my childhood. Nothing indicated to her that letting a kid mix up her OshKosh B'gosh overalls and tops and wear six scrunchies at a time and hog the bathroom mirror could pave her way forward in any way.

But here we are.

I spend a good portion of my day in front of my bathroom mirror with my camera going, talking to millions of people. It's important that I use my imagination when I'm talking to all those people so I can see them in my mind. To think about how I can help them and what would be interesting to them. It's as though Castanada and Jelly (and the occasional Mr. Jelly) are back in my life.

And it's all real.

. . .

I admit it. I'm a word nerd.

I love words that capture a feeling perfectly. I love words that have melodic sounds. I love words that are unexpected.

For example, take the word *apricate*.

Want to guess what it means?

It means "to bask in the sun." Come on, that word is a winner. Not that I'm planning to use it in a conversation anytime soon. But still.

Want a classier word for *hashtag*? You know, #?

Octothorpe, that's what. I seriously want to start using this one on my social platforms. *Be sure and tag us at octothorpe arealgoodlife!*

Okay, let's do one more. *Imparadise.*

How poetic is that? It's a verb, and it means to make someone blissfully happy, to create a state of joy. And that sounds like something we'd probably all want to experience as part of the good life—times that are happy, silly, fun, and sweet for ourselves and for the people living alongside us.

Maybe it's because I was raised in a family that spoke two languages, or maybe it's because of media training, but words have always held a fascination for me. Think about it: We take this string of sounds and symbols, we arrange and rearrange them into patterns, and we all then somehow agree that they mean something. Think about the word *blue*. What pops up in your mind when you read those symbols? The color, right? And you probably also then thought about the emotion of feeling blue—feeling a little down or sad. Four symbols, lined up a certain way, and together they carry this meaning of color and emotion.

Two of my very favorite words are *Valentina* and *Amari*. Yes, it's because those are my girls' names. But they're my girls' names because I love how soft and rich those names sound. I love what their names mean. *Valentina* means "healthy and strong." *Amari* means "promised by God." Before I knew my girls, I knew the legacy I wanted them to receive, that of health and strength and the promises of God. We began speaking those names over the girls before they were born, and once they were born, those names, those collections of sounds and letters, have come to mean even more. If my name wasn't Sazan, I'd want it to be my girls' names.

There's tremendous power in the words we say, the words we choose to speak over ourselves, our lives, and our days. In the Kurdish community where I grew up, we were all big talkers. We use lots and lots of words to describe simple events. We add all kinds of verbal flair to stories.

But as much as I love words, I haven't always been careful with them. Especially the words I've spoken over myself.

I was tough on myself as a kid.

I was tough on myself as a teenager.

I was tough on myself when I started my career.

And I was especially tough on myself amid the changes I saw in the mirror during my pregnancy with Teeny.*

I'd pick apart anything I didn't think was perfect. I'd scold myself for the dimples showing up on my tush, and I'd grumble at my emerging double chin. I'd grumble about the extra curl and frizz in my hair, and I'd freak if my hair looked too flat. I even became critical of my knuckles, noting how swollen they looked in the mirror and on camera.

I was saying all this stuff to myself—in my head and in the mirror.

And in my heart.

---

* This didn't change much after I had Teeny, and that season inspired the Makeup & Motivate series on my YouTube channel. Starting this series helped me to connect more deeply with myself and with God in my early days of motherhood. Search "Just Be You" on https://www.youtube.com/sazanhendrix to see that first video and hear the story behind Makeup & Motivate.

Getting lost in the rabbit hole of weight and body comparison was something I struggled with most of the pregnancy. I didn't understand what my body was doing, which made trusting the process so hard for me. I spent a lot of days dwelling on the unknowns, and I let anxiety rob the peace and joy in my journey.

It was at our baby shower for Teeny, when I was almost nine months pregnant, that a memory about words helped me heal.

The baby shower was held at our home in Los Angeles. It was the sweetest celebration, getting ready for our daughter to come into the world. One of my favorite parts of the shower was when everyone gathered in the living room with Stevie and me after eating and opening gifts. And one by one, each person gave us their best advice, sharing the wisdom they had collected from their families and their experiences. They spoke words of hope and words of blessing, giving their best advice for the soon-to-be mama and daddy.

Something came over me when it came time for my mom to speak. Maybe it was the hormones. But there was also something so raw and time-bending about getting ready to welcome my daughter into the world while sitting with my mom. Memories came flooding back to me, flashbacks of how much my mom had sacrificed when I was little. How much she had to deal with in raising a very sassy, determined, strong-willed child like me.

Something just clicked at that moment with my own daughter in utero. I was getting all this amazing advice about raising my daughter, but I realized that some of the best knowledge I already had was about how my mom raised me. Before my mom could add her voice to the circle, I had to get something off my chest.

"Mom." I trembled, pushing through the coming tears. "There's something in this moment that I'm just coming to know. Never once in my childhood, as difficult as I was every time I looked in the mirror, every time I wanted to pick myself apart with those bangs, when I was freaking out and re-brushing my hair and having a fit, not once can I remember you speaking ill of yourself as you were getting yourself ready. Never. Not once to this day."

She never picked herself apart in front of me.

She never picked me apart.

My mom would never tell you she has it all together or that she's never dealt with insecurities or doubts. But in front of me, in front of the mirror, she never called herself fat, never said she hated her nose, and never complained about her hair. She decided when she became a mom that she wouldn't bully herself in front of her daughters. She decided she would be intentional with how she reacted to her greatest fears.

And now, as I was getting ready to welcome my own daughter, I realized for the first time what a gift that was to me.

Later, I asked her how. How did she manage to do this? She said, "I never gave negative talk the permission to speak lies over me." She also said, "It's amazing how your children can become the biggest inspiration behind why you choose to love and accept the way you are. If you can't do it for yourself, do it for them."

· · ·

Who do you talk to in the mirror when you start your day? And what words do you use?

Look, it's pretty impossible to build a good day and a good life if you're using harsh, negative, painful words as your mortar. I find that we women make it all too easy to speak terrible things over ourselves. We even say awful things about ourselves to each other. My friend will tell me my skin looks good, and I'll tell her I've got a zit ready to go nuclear. Stevie will compliment how I look in a pair of jeans, and I'll tell him the reasons I need to hit it harder in the gym. What is up with that?

Here's what I know.

When Teeny and I stand in front of the mirror together every morning, when I'm making my meditation the long strokes through her hair, I would never say critical words to her. So why do I say them to myself?

Owning this one day and finding the good in my life is based on loving the way God made me. It's knowing that I can still speak life and gratitude instead of criticism, even amid the insecurities, chaos, horrible haircuts, and bad hair days. I want my daughter to look into the mirror and know God made her special—that nobody else in the world looks like her. That her DNA is unique to her. God created her, me, my mother, and everybody else reading this book to be special and different.

> **It's pretty impossible to build a good day and a good life if you're using harsh, negative, painful words as your mortar.**

There is something so special in knowing that God said, "I'm going to make so many children to walk on this earth, but they're each going to be unique. They're not going to look alike; even identical twins will have differences that make them unique, even to their fingerprints." I think God did this with the intention of reminding us that he doesn't want us to be like anyone else; otherwise, he could have just cloned us and gotten on with it.

A verse that is really important to me comes to mind. There was a king in Israel long ago named David. He was not only a king, but also a musician and a songwriter. He wrote Psalm 119, and check this out. Tradition says he wrote Psalm 119 to teach the Hebrew ABCs to his son Solomon. Rabbis say it wasn't only just to help him memorize the letters but also to teach him the "alphabet of the spiritual life."[1] And right in the middle of that psalm is this line: "Your hands made me and formed me" (v. 73).

It feels like David's moment in the mirror with his son, when David reminds Solomon that he is God's unique creation. It's fundamental. It's powerful.

David also went on to write these words in Psalm 139: "For you created my inmost being; you knit me together in my mother's womb. I praise you because I am fearfully and wonderfully made; your works are wonderful, I know that full well" (vv. 13–14).

To be able to honestly tell Teeny that she is wonderful, that she is unique, that she is exactly who God designed her to be, I have to be able to speak it over myself. You can be one of the most encouraging people in the world to your friends, family, and coworkers, but if you can't believe and speak good over yourself, you can't fully believe it for the people you love.

What will influence generations to come all starts this morning in this bathroom with what I say. It starts with my dramatic five-year-old who's giving me the hairstyle request of the day and who's complaining about her hair not being perfect. In that moment, how I choose to react and respond can make all the difference. As I brush Teeny's hair in the mornings, I'm reminded again that how my mom treated herself in front of me needs to be what Teeny sees and hears me do.

I want Teeny to grow up and know that, while her mother wasn't perfect, she saw me speak good in the midst of chaos. I want her to think about the times I asked her for forgiveness when I lost it and had my mommy meltdowns. I want her to remember me walking in humility.

I also want her to remember that her mom, just like her grandmother, never said anything bad about herself in front of her as a child. She can carry that for generations to come.

If you're a mom, watch how you talk to yourself in the mirror—both the mirror that reflects our physical image and the mirror of comparison and opinion we often find ourselves in front of. If you're not yet a mom, it doesn't mean the next generation of girls isn't watching; they are. What are you saying in front of other women? What are you saying about other women? What are you saying about yourself?

Are you criticizing your body? Are you saying things about your body shape, your stretch marks, or the physical challenges you are experiencing?

Does that negative voice tell you that you're not measuring up? Does it point out every "flaw" on your face? Does it bring up all kinds of points of comparison that leave you feeling flat?

I like to use this visual on my mirror to remind me about what I say to myself. I take Post-it Notes and write down declarations for myself. Then I stick them on my mirror and say them out loud each day while I get ready. Sure, you may have already heard of people doing this kind of thing. But here's where I want you to take it a step further.

Write down what you're not even sure you believe about yourself yet. Struggling with your body image? Write:

- "I love my curvy body."
- "I am fearfully and wonderfully made."
- "I am thankful for these stretch marks that brought me my kids."
- "I am thankful for this body that is working through the challenge of fertility issues."

Finding that you have a hard time moving away from criticizing yourself? Write:

- "I am exactly who I am supposed to be."
- "I love myself."
- "I love my smile."
- "I love making people laugh."
- "I love that I make other people feel comfortable."
- "God is for me."

Writing down your declarations sends an important message to your mind. The very act of writing them, even the ones that seem a little hard to believe right now, interrupts some of those negative thought patterns. And then, each morning as you read these declarations to yourself, your mind gets the opportunity to hear you, in your own voice, owning and adapting the narrative. It really does help change the voice in your head and what it says about you, to you.

I hope it includes the encouragement and the truth that you are wonderful. That you are beautifully you.

I also want you to ask yourself these three questions when you feel that critical voice rising:

1. **IS IT TRUE?** We repeat all kinds of weird little lies to ourselves. "My hips are disgusting." Really? Come on. Hips aren't disgusting. Limiting beauty standards are. Don't believe everything you tell yourself, particularly when the critical voice is talking.

2. **WHO SAID IT?** I'm shocked at times when I find myself echoing a mean comment or a hurtful statement from someone long ago. Why should I make someone else's opinion of me my inner voice? If it's something God says about me, then I want to listen. If it's something someone said out of ignorance or mean-spiritedness or even just a different opinion, those words don't need to come clouding my inner dialogue.

3. **IS IT HORMONES OR THAT TIME OF THE MONTH?** Seriously. I really have noticed that at certain times of the month, I tend to hear the inner critic more loudly. And when I chart it on a calendar, there it is: that hormonal hot topic. Don't underestimate how your monthly cycles can unleash the critical beast. Stay aware of how your physiological calendar influences what you say to yourself and when.

Speak hurt, and you'll grow hurt.

Speak good, and you'll grow good.

My mama said it best: "When you're unhappy with what you see, pretend there is a little girl watching who wants to be just like you. Don't let her down."

MIDDAY
FOCUS

I (Sazan) have heard people say they are morning people. Some folks in my life even say they are part of the five a.m. club (I'm looking at you, Jon Volk!). And I've heard other people say they are night owls. They get that late-night jolt of energy and do things like repainting their living room at midnight.

But I don't think I've ever heard anyone claim to be a midday person.

There's the afternoon slump and the afternoon nap.

The midday espresso.

That's about it when it comes to how people think about the middle part of the day.

But when it comes to living your good life, midday is when a whole lot of the action happens. For a lot of us, those are the hours when we dig into work, when we learn, when we move forward in our pursuit of our careers and callings.

> In between waking up from bed in the morning and going back in the evening, let something happen. God will bless that "something" for you.[1]
>
> —Israelmore Ayivor

There it is, the most obvious portion of the day, right in the middle of the clock. But it's the time of day we can underestimate. Decisions or challenges that come up during midday can have me tossing and turning at midnight. If I'm not focused on my priorities in midday, it pushes the to-do list into the next day and the next.

When I think about the rhythm of a day, *focus* is the mascot for midday.

Back when the Romans were running the world, the word *focus* in Latin meant your hearth or fireplace, the center of the home.[2] Which is why, over time, *focus* also came to mean "home." That just blows me away—that when I'm talking about staying focused, the very word reminds me of this home I'm building, of this life I'm constructing minute by minute.

Those midday hours drive a lot of our work and our to-do list. A good life includes those things we do to support our families, as well as stuff like keeping everybody in clean clothes. Midday to me feels like the practical friend in the circle of times of the day. It's when the things get done.

And if your focus strays during these precious hours, it can be all too easy to grind your way through urgent and small stuff but lose sight of the important things. So much flies at us during midday, from jumping into that meeting to trying to get to our kid's preschool on time for pickup. We have emails to answer and house repairs to schedule. Last-minute project updates and the realization that we don't have that one ingredient we need to make dinner.

When Stevie and I talk with people who have some big vision in their lives but are struggling to make it happen, I'm always curious to hear about what they do from lunch forward. I love it when people tell me about their morning routines, setting up the day. But that morning intention is realized through the course of the afternoon. The pace you set for the day needs to find steadiness as the hours go by.

When focus drifts during the afternoon, when your energy drops and your distractions grow, what then?

Yes, we talked about gaze strategy in a previous chapter, helping us reflect on where we want to go. But now I want you to get more specific, to learn how to not just look where you want to head but to really zoom in, get clear about the details. I'm excited to share with you some things we've learned when it comes to how we spend our midday. Midday is probably the time of day for me that needs the most flexibility right now. It's the time of day when I have to reevaluate often, to make sure it's working the way it needs to for our business and our kids. During this portion of the clock, a whole lot of activity and creativity gets crammed in as we work around our girls' schedules.

That flexibility, it's really part of how to focus. When my eyes are trying to focus on something, my lenses change shape to bring whatever I'm looking at into focus. And that's how it is with these important midday hours. At times I have to change the shape of my expectations. Other times I have to change the shape of just how much I think I can get done. The babysitter cancels, the repairman shows up, the call gets canceled. To stay focused, I have to adjust the lens through which I'm looking at the day.

So I've decided to use a lens that stays on the things I've said are important. There's a lens that I sometimes am tempted to use, one that focuses on what has gone off the rails during the day or one that homes in on a particularly tough conversation or interaction. When that happens, my focus carries me off on all kinds of trails that aren't productive. But when I use my lens of seeing the tasks of the day through a focus of good, of gratitude, of curiosity, of learning, it's pretty incredible how much still gets done in spite of distractions.

Don't let the distractions of midday pull you away from the things that bring you closer to your purpose. With so much pulling at you, it can all look like a blur—believe me, I know! But pick one thing, even if it's just getting your sink cleared or writing that one email. Focus on it for five minutes. Take a breath. Then choose what you're going to focus on next. You and me, we get closer to our dreams one task and one day at a time.

CHAPTER 5

FOCUS ON OPENING YOUR EYES TO SEE

Everywhere he looked, things were bad.

And not just in the *inconvenient* or *things-not-going-your-way* kinds of bad.

No, this kind of bad was warfare. Geopolitical upheaval.

Genocide.

My grandfather knew it was time to get out—time to leave all he had known. He'd fought. He'd endured. He had put his neck on the line, and not just in a symbolic sense. There was a warrant out for him to be captured and hung, literally, by the neck.

If he was going to survive this, if his wife and children were going to survive this, he had to get them out. And that would mean completely starting over.

I (Sazan) am Kurdish on both sides of my family, by birth and by culture. All my family speaks Kurdish, the language of my people, and we have traditions and customs that are a thousand years old. Growing up Kurdish is powerful. It's deep-rooted. It's family. It's about generosity and extravagant hospitality toward others. It's about glorious food and family gatherings that last until the early morning hours. It's being part of a collection of family and friends that are all up in each other's business because they love and care for each other so much. In America, it's an immigrant community that has seen hard times and horrible events, and being pilgrims together makes the bonds even stronger.

The Kurdish people have a vibrant and complicated history. Originally, our people lived in the mountains of what's now northern Iraq, Iran, Syria, Armenia, and eastern Turkey. It's an area known as Kurdistan, and the culture of the land is ancient. One of our most famous leaders in history is Saladin. He reigned over the Kurds in the twelfth century. He was brilliant and ambitious, and he expanded the Kurdish kingdom to include parts of Egypt, Iraq, and North Africa. Through the next several centuries, the Kurds would become part of the Ottoman Empire.

By the early part of the twentieth century, things had started to shift. After World War I, as part of the Treaty of Sèvres, the Kurds were supposed to be given their own independent state. But that's not the way it went down. Instead, the Kurdish people and lands were split up. We're now a people without a home, as you'll notice Kurdistan isn't on the map. We're a community that has been pushed out of its rightful place. Territorial wars and horrible crimes against the Kurdish people have been taking place over the last century. The Kurds no longer have a state, a place to call their own.

Enter Saddam Hussein, the extremist Iraqi dictator responsible for a half-million deaths and countless human rights abuses. In the 1970s, he started coming against the Kurds to expand Iraq. That's how my other grandfather, my dad's dad, died. My dad was only eight years old when his dad was tortured and killed, a martyr for the Kurds. To this day, we have no grave to visit to honor him. And through those later years, my family continued to lose countless friends and relatives in brutal mass killings under Saddam Hussein's regime.

If you speak with any Kurdish person today, they will have similar stories to share. The stories have bonded us in a painful way; our people have been slaughtered, misrepresented, and—oftentimes in the world's view—become invisible and forgotten. Even after Saddam, we have continued to fight for our freedom as a community and culture.

The Kurdish people joined the fight to protect their families and homes in many ways. Some joined the Kurdish *peshmerga*. It was a small independent group fighting against enemy forces, and the name *peshmerga* means "those who face death." Both of my grandfathers were peshmerga—one dying for the cause, and the other bearing the scar of a bullet wound for the rest of his life. Other people stood their ground in passive resistance. Others spoke out publicly against what was happening.

That's when things got even more horrible. Saddam Hussein started using chemical weapons against the Kurds as punishment for their stand for independence. He killed close to two hundred thousand Kurdish men, women, and children in the Anfal campaign—a genocide—of 1988. My maiden name is Barzani. The Kurdish Barzani tribe is my extended family group. Eight thousand Barzanis were taken and killed during Anfal. My dad's younger brother was supposed to be among those who were kidnapped. When the soldiers arrived to grab him, he wasn't home because he was out running an errand and was able to evade them. He was spared, but so many other tribe members were slaughtered. Their bodies were dumped in mass unmarked graves. People known for having spoken out against Saddam's regime were rounded up and killed. Over one million Kurds were moved into horrific camps.

By the 1970s, my mom's dad, the grandfather we called Bawka, knew his life was on the line. Bawka used an unlikely weapon to fight the injustice against the Kurdish people. He used a paintbrush.

While we grandkids knew him as Bawka, to the Kurdish people, he was the celebrated painter Jamal Bekhtyar. He was known for his beautiful portraits and use of vivid color. He'd built a whole career capturing the beauty of the Kurdish experience and painting the faces of the Kurdish people. And then he'd turned his paintbrush toward the story of the oppression and violence the Kurdish people were facing. His paintings captured the heartbreak and slaughter that was happening.

For that, Saddam Hussein wanted my grandfather to hang.

What strikes me when I look at my grandfather's paintings today is how beautiful they are. Some of them are hard to look at because of the stories they tell. Somehow my grandfather was able to render the events experienced by my people under Saddam Hussein's regime with vibrant color and skilled strokes. He seemed to see the brutality of what was happening to the Kurdish people while also magnificently showing their power and courage. Somehow, in the midst of so many things that were incredibly bad, Bawka was able to represent the beauty that fought back. Through his gorgeous, disturbing paintings, he opened the eyes of people around the world to the plight of the Kurdish people.

What a gift, to be able to see what's wrong in the world as well as what's right in it—and what *could* be right in it.

Whenever I enter a Kurdish home today, there are a few things I know I'll find. A beautiful plate of dates and nuts on the coffee table to welcome me. A cup of hot, spicy-sweet cardamom tea to refresh me. And a copy of one of my grandfather's paintings on the wall, reminding me of my heritage as a Kurd and of my legacy as the granddaughter of a man who found color and beauty and truth amid some of the hardest circumstances.

Bawka's work, without words, speaks in an instant.

While my grandfather suffered political exile and had to fight as a peshmerga against the Ba'ath regime, my grandmother and her children had to stay behind as refugees until they could reunite. Once she was able, my grandmother rounded up her children and walked with them for three days to reach the camp. By the time she arrived, she and the children were desperately ill, to the point it was uncertain how many of them would survive.

Ultimately, Bawka and my grandmother were able to bring their family to the United States in 1976. My grandfather knew he wanted to come to the United States because he wanted his children to experience what he felt was most important—the opportunity for education. They settled first in Bismarck, North Dakota, and a few years later moved to Nashville, Tennessee, where they lived in community surrounded by other Kurds escaping the conflict back home. My grandparents finally settled in a small home in San Diego, California. Their children would go on to earn degrees and build lives that spanned their Kurdish upbringing and their American experience.

As a little girl, I loved to visit my grandparents in San Diego. My grandfather's studio was in their garage. Bawka would raise the door of the garage, turn on a fan to softly move the coastal breeze, and set to work. He'd show me how to mix his paint colors on the palette, adding a dab of green to the black to deepen the color, adding rose to a blue to pull out a more vibrant shade. He always was a snappy dresser, and his hands were so elegant as he blended the tints. He'd move to the canvas, and I'd watch him layer on the colors, his brushstrokes sometimes tiny and careful, other times sweeping and dramatic.

With his brush, he conducted an orchestra of history—a symphony of good, hard truth.

Through the years I've wondered how he could still paint beauty while so clearly seeing the cruelty that humans can inflict on one another.

Not all of his work was centered on the atrocities committed on the Kurdish people. He also painted lush landscapes and gorgeous portraits of women. He did a series of monochromatic paintings of several of his new country's monuments, such as the Washington Monument and the Jefferson Memorial. Somehow, some way, Bawka was able to create compelling messages about *all* the experiences of his life. Somehow, he was always able to see the good.

. . .

Part of the good life is having good vision. Good vision is, sure, about focus. It's about looking in the direction you're headed. But it's also bigger than that. It's about deciding what you're going to see and how you're going to think about it.

Before Bawka passed at the age of ninety-five, a meme about a dress was making its way around social media. Do you remember that one? It was a picture of a dress with broad stripes, and the image didn't even really show the whole dress. But for a moment, it was the most famous dress of the season. Its fabric or cut or design weren't remarkable. What made it the talk of the town was that no one could agree on its color.

> It's about deciding what you're going to see and how you're going to think about it.

It was wild, and the issue sparked really crazy online debates. Some people saw the stripes on the dress as gold and white, and other people saw them as black and blue. (Stevie and I were on opposite sides of the dress debate, even though I was right.)

So what was going on there? How could so many of us see the same picture and yet see it in different colors? How could that even be a thing?

Journalists, scientists, and even ophthalmologists ended up getting in on the conversation to try to develop an explanation. As it turns out, there is a brain phenomenon that explains why we had different experiences seeing the same thing. It's called top-down processing.

What's top-down processing? I won't pretend to be a neuroscientist, but in a nutshell, top-down processing is the phenomenon that we see what our brain tells us it *expects* to see. So if your friend told you to look at the picture of the gold-and-white dress that everyone was talking about, you'd already be primed to see a gold-and-white dress.

Some scientists decided another factor was also at work—something called color constancy. We don't *just* see color. Our brains take in the surroundings and the lighting, which influence the way we see color.

Can I just tell you, any time I choose paint for a room, I will pick a swatch at the paint store that looks like the perfect creamy white, and by the time I get home and tape that swatch up on the wall, all of a sudden it looks more green or pink or blue. Has that happened to you? (To go even further, have you pulled the Sazan method of going ahead and painting the whole room, only to discover that—surprise!—that perfect white still looks green? Go figure.)

So when it comes to seeing that meme dress as white and gold or blue and black, your brain does this amazing thing. Even though you can't observe the lighting or the surroundings in which that original picture of the dress was taken, your brain will fill in the details anyway. *Then* your brain will decide whether you see gold and white or black and blue.[1]

How. Wild. Is. That.

What does this mean for the good life? Friend, if you expect to see good in your life, then you'll see good. And if you decide the events surrounding your life are *for* your good and are paths that will ultimately lead to opportunity and joy and satisfaction, then your life will take on the hue of goodness.

At times you will have to look hard for the good. Really hard. Opening your eyes to see is a decision. It's a skill. It's a practice. It's being an artist. I want to be careful here, to make sure you understand I'm not telling you to deny reality or to refuse to stare down anything ugly or difficult. That stuff is out there, and we have to deal with it.

This kind of seeing is not about pretending that bad doesn't exist or that crappy situations don't happen. It's not about maniacally proclaiming that everything is *fine, just fine*, when life is on fire. What it is about is looking for what can be learned, gleaned, and experienced for your ultimate good. It's about finding the color of life when everything looks dark.

> At times you will have to look hard for the good.

What we've learned as parents and as business owners is that days start as an empty canvas. And just like my grandfather, we have to decide what colors and shapes we are going to use to fill the canvases of our days. I think of our calendar as a canvas: What am I filling those hours with? Do I see beauty there? Did I include margin to pause and notice what is around me?

Stevie and I remind each other in gray seasons to do two things: to look up and to look out. And here's what we mean by that. To look up is to look up to God. We might not always understand a tough season we're going through, but when we look up to God, we're reminded of his love and his presence, even amidst the hard times.

To look out means to look beyond ourselves, to think about others and how to love them well. It's all too easy in a difficult time to only look inward—to focus on what's missing, what we're failing at, what's lacking. But when we look out, we stop focusing on ourselves and can see with fresh eyes.

Looking hard for the good can start with finding one thing. Your favorite cozy blanket you're wrapped in while reading this. The tree that's starting to change color just beyond your apartment balcony. Like my grandfather working on one of his paintings, take a step back and look at what you're coloring your life with. Check the proportions. Are you making too much of little annoyances? Are you minimizing the color and life you *can* see? Each day, your life is a fresh canvas. Choose the colors for your paint palette thoughtfully. Because whether you mean to or not, you are painting the portrait of your life.

.   .   .

There is a Kurdish documentary about my Bawka. It features some pictures of him as a young man, sitting at a river, talking with friends, as well as another picture of him during his time as a peshmerga. There are photos of him in later life, painting in his studio in the garage in San Diego. Snapshots of him holding grandchildren.

He never stopped making people aware of the Kurdish cause. He was exceptionally generous, often giving away his paintings to people who admired them. And he used his brush for good, right up to the end.

I want to have eyes like Bawka. Somehow, in the midst of darkness, he was able to fix his eyes on hope's light. He kept looking for a way to get his family out from under Saddam Hussein's crushing evil. He saw brightness when life seemed to only be serving up black coal. He could find the color in the murky depths. His example makes me think of Matthew 6:22: "The eye is the lamp of the body. If your eyes are healthy, your whole body will be full of light." Bawka was asked by a friend one time what his favorite color was to paint with. True to form, he said he loved all the colors—that each one had a story to tell, the rainbow captured on canvas.

There's a type of fish that's known throughout Kurdistan. The fish isn't considered all that exotic, but its scales shimmer like a rainbow when it comes to the surface of the water. In English, we'd think of it as a carp. Goldfish, in all their varieties, are part of the carp family. This fish reminds me of what my grandfather could do with his art, bringing forth color, gold and shimmer, a glimmer of the rainbow in the darkest of waters.

The Kurdish word for that kind of fish is *sazan*. My name.

Bawka saw something in me. It was Bawka who left me a legacy of beauty and Kurdish pride and artistic devotion. He taught me so much about seeing the good, even in the hard. After all, he's the one who named me.

It was Bawka who named me Sazan.

CHAPTER 6

FOCUS ON GETTING COMFORTABLE WITH CHAOS

O ne day, midday, Sazan and I had a fight.
A big one.

Maybe the biggest fight we've ever had.

Okay. The biggest.

It was the fall of 2019. We had just sold our house in Los Angeles, and we were desperately searching for a new home. As much as we tried over months and months, we just couldn't find the next house that would be our home. I remember going to at least a hundred open houses and thinking, *Will this be* another *no?*

We moved back to Texas for the summer to live with my family as the house hunt continued, our plans in disarray. One day, I sat with my brother, talking about the difficulties we were having. He said, "You know, you guys really could be anywhere. You've got this time with no mortgage; that's like the ultimate freedom! If your work hasn't slowed down since you've been in Texas, you could really work from wherever. If I were you, I would go to Europe."

Wait. What?

I would love to go to Europe! That would be the dream! As his advice bounced around in my brain, a plan began to form.

"Look, that would be incredible. But you've gotta help me out here. Somehow, we've got to get Sazan on board with this, and you're a way better negotiator than I am. You could sell rocks to a caveman. Help me put together a pitch to Sazan."

We strategized for a while. I knew that if I were the one to bring this idea up to my beautiful and practical wife, it didn't stand a great chance. But I also knew that if my brother were the one to toss it out there, it might just have a shot. Probably a one-in-a-million shot, but that would be better than my one-in-the-backside-of-never chance.

My brother gave the performance of a lifetime at dinner. With the three of us sitting at the table, he casually brought up travel and how much we love it. Sazan immediately stepped into his circle, enthusiastically talking about her favorite places we'd been. That's when he sprung like a cobra.

Except, you know, subtle-like.

"You know, you guys don't even have a mortgage right now. You should just go to Europe for a month . . ."

My wife looked at him and laughed. "Ha ha. No way."

I looked at her, an innocent expression on my conniving face. "I mean, we could," I added, wide-eyed. "We don't have a house payment, so we don't have a house to worry about. The house hunting has come up zeros. Why don't we just go?"

That was the breakthrough moment. Instead of Sazan coming right back at me with a *There's no way we're going to Europe, Stevie. Leave it alone*, she sat back in her chair and thought.

"You know . . ." she paused a moment to ponder the idea. "Maybe we could."

And that's when my dream started becoming a reality.

. . .

To go to Europe for a month was something I never thought I'd get to do in my lifetime. When I was a kid, my family didn't get to travel that often. I remember our extended families would have to pitch in so we could travel to see them in Maryland and California. Those family reunion trips, when we went to the airport, felt like the biggest adventure in the world. I was so excited every time I got to fly, and as I got older, my passion for travel only grew stronger. To be able to go in this season of my life with my wife and Teeny, who was two years old at the time, was simply incredible.

As we started pulling our plans together, we filled them with dreams of days spent hanging out together, drinking beer, climbing mountains, eating good food, laughing, and speaking Italian. Then we boarded a plane and did the thing.

It started out as everything I'd hoped for. The sights were incredible. The culture was fascinating. It was great.

Except a confusing chaos of emotions was chasing me.

My negotiator brother and I were able to catch up by phone on our third stop in the south of France. "How's it going?" his voice rang out over the phone line, full of excitement and curiosity.

"You know, good, good . . ."

He heard the hesitancy in my voice. "What's up, Stevie?"

"Well, I hate to say this. And I know this is what I really wanted, and we're so fortunate to be able to do this. But . . ."

"But what?" he asked.

I sighed. "I just really want to come home," I confessed.

"Why on earth would you want to come home from your European vacation?" He chuckled, disbelief in his tone.

"You know, we've been searching for a home for so long, and being here . . . well, it reminds me that more than anything, I just really want to find a home. I hate saying it because this is the trip of a lifetime. It's confusing. But that's how it is," I told him.

It was. I was bewildered. I'd wanted this. And now my feelings were upside down. It made no sense.

This had been a particularly stress-free trip, which only compounded my sense of guilt over my confession to my brother. Someone had already booked our hotels for us and done a great job finding some top-of-the-line locations. Everything was going so smoothly; we didn't even have to worry about where we were staying or any other kinds of details.

That is, until we drove from Provence to Nice in France.

That drive took several hours, and Teeny was more than ready to get out of the car. Heck, I was too. The area where our next hotel was located was in a very busy part of town, and I had to battle the traffic and confusing directions.

Hotels in France don't always have the wide circular drives and close parking lots we're used to here in the United States. At this particular hotel in Nice, we had to park away from the hotel and pull all our luggage out of the car and down this narrow little street. We hustled our bags and our toddler for a couple of blocks until we reached the entrance to the hotel. I went up to the registration desk and gave our name and reservation number, eager to get checked in and upstairs.

After some clicking around on her computer, the reservations agent regarded me with an apologetic smile. "I'm sorry, Mr. Hendrix," she said in a beautiful accent. "But I don't see any reservation for you here. Are you sure this is the right hotel?"

Um, yeah, I'm sure. I had my handy-dandy reservations folder that our travel agent had given us right in my sweaty hand.

"Look again," I encouraged her. "I'm sure this is the place."

Her manicured fingers flew across the keyboard again. She squinted at her screen, tapped on a few more keys, then met my eyes. "No, sir, I'm sorry. There's an entry with your name, but it shows that your reservation was canceled. And we don't have any more rooms available."

Well, just French-freaking-fantastic.

We hadn't had any lunch. We'd just hauled luggage with a hungry, grumpy toddler in tow over two blocks of narrow cobblestone streets. And now we were high and dry with no place to stay.

I curtly thanked the hotel clerk and dug my cell phone out of my pocket.

"Hello!" answered the travel agent back in the States, all sunshine and smiles.

I explained the situation to her.

"Oh, yes, I booked you into an Airbnb that I thought you'd like better! Sounds like you didn't get the update!"

Sounds like I didn't get the update? Uh, yeah.

She gave me the address for the Airbnb she had booked for us, and we headed back down the street. We piled our luggage into the back of the car, then Teeny started wailing when we strapped her back into her car seat. Sazan was stewing at a low simmer. I got behind the wheel and started driving through the twisting, tight streets, frustrated that the agent had booked this Airbnb without getting my approval. Who knew what we were walking into?

The deeper we drove into Nice, the tinier the roads became. I had rented a Dodge Durango for this trip, a full-on American-sized SUV.

Here's something I learned: Full-sized SUVs were not designed to navigate twisty-turny alleyways that pretend to be streets in Europe. I was flustered by this sudden change in plans and even more flustered by trying to get down these hallways of roads.

Next to me in the passenger seat, Sazan started offering a narrative. "Why would they book us something different without even telling us? Do you even know where we are going? Watch out for that curb! Are we going to be able to get all our luggage in there, or will we have to hike to this place too? What about Teeny? Will she have a bed? What if there are nine flights of stairs up to the place we're going to stay? How are we going to get all our stuff up a flight of stairs while also trying to carry Teeny? Look out for that car!"

My blood pressure was going through the roof, and I was pretty sure steam was starting to rise off my brain.

"How could you not have known about this?" Sazan continued. "If you weren't staying on top of your email or messages, this is your fault."

I gripped the steering wheel, trying to keep the car from brushing up against the buildings that were inches from either side of the vehicle. "Saz, I need you to calm down. We'll get this all figured out once I get us out of this crazy cobblestone shaft."

"But I don't understand how you could let this hap—"

And then I blew.

Like . . . *blew* blew. Boiling point reached, lava pouring over.

"Shut up!" I screamed. "Shut up, shut up, shut up!" I shouted the same phrase probably ten more times.

The best part? Our two-year-old sat in the back of the car, hearing every bit of this.

Yeah. What a proud moment.

We'd never had a fight that furious, never torn at each other verbally that viciously before.

And we managed to do it over a modified hotel reservation in one of the most beautiful places in the world, amid a vacation experience few people get to have.

That's when I learned this: Chaos will come and find you. He will bang on your door, and you, unexpecting, will always answer it, like, "I didn't know you were coming back!"

Chaos responds, "Well, you can't escape me. I come at any time, any season, anywhere, any hour."

Up until that afternoon with Sazan, I'd actually been thinking to myself that she and I had been getting along really well on this trip despite the stress of the past few months.

Now, I know better.

That's exactly when Chaos likes to strike. Chaos can take a simple stressor, a small miscommunication, and turn it into a full-on stress fest.

Were we living the good life by being on this trip together? Yes.

Were we living the good life, being able to make plans to move closer to friends and family? Yes.

Were we living the good life, able to take our work with us and continue our business remotely? Also yes.

Did that mean Chaos was going to leave us alone?

No.

Chaos can arrive like a tank, guns blazing. Or he can tear through your roof like a runaway meteorite. But Chaos can also come in small and wreak all kinds of havoc, like a silent assault of termites. Either way, he's there to do damage. He's there to destroy.

He can make you question—deeply question—if you have any kind of good life at all.

.   .   .

In February 2021, we had a crazy weather event here in Austin, Texas. It came to be known as Snowpocalypse. I've also heard it called Snowvid, another clever quip. It's not that we had feet of snow never known before in the western hemisphere. Nope. We got some serious inches, but nothing that, say, the good people of Michigan wouldn't call an average Saturday afternoon.

But here, it brought the whole city to a standstill. Heck, practically the whole state.

The electrical grid was completely overwhelmed. Roads were iced in and blocked for days. The city water system was plagued by burst pipes and frozen lines.

What happened?

Well, our fair city is used to fair weather, and it's pretty pleasant most of the time. Because of that, we just don't plan for storms like this. We don't have reserves set aside in case a winter system moves into our good winter days. And then, when some snow falls, the whole place falls apart.

I learned during Snowvid to keep extra water bottles, a generator, and some cans of tuna on hand. I don't want to get caught like that again. And I've gotten comfortable with the fact that some climate chaos is bound to show up from time to time. It doesn't mean I need to be panicked about it. It doesn't mean I need to build a bunker in the backyard beneath Teeny and Amari's playhouse. What it does mean is that part of living in a place with good weather means I've got to be okay when the weather turns. It doesn't mean this isn't a good place to live.

We can get lulled into thinking Chaos has retired when we experience a long run of easy days. Or we can assume chaos is all there is when we experience a tough season.

But really, Chaos is simply our neighbor. Granted, not the best neighbor. He loves to throw trash over the fence. His dogs, Tumult and Snarl, sometimes bark through the night. And he comes over at the most inconvenient times, ready to crash the family get-together or interrupt what had been a delightful day.

Sometimes he even shows up on your European vacation.

I'm learning to make peace with him. For a long time, I wanted to deny Chaos's presence. But to keep my peace, I have to acknowledge that Chaos will be part of my good life. It's like what my spiritual teacher, Jesus, had to say: "I have told you these things, so that in me you may have peace. In this world you will have trouble. But take heart! I have overcome the world" (John 16:33).

After our horrible blowup, Sazan and I decided we had to get comfortable with Chaos. Doing so protects our marriage. It helps us deal with unexpected delays and challenges. We've made keeping our peace, individually and in our relationship, a big priority. We don't let Chaos speak for us when stress begins to rise.

> To keep my peace, I have to acknowledge that Chaos will be part of my good life.

How do we do that? Sometimes we need to go old-school and put ourselves in time-out. Yep, time-out. When you feel your emotions of overwhelm or irritation rising, sit 'em in the corner for a bit. It doesn't mean you're not acknowledging how you feel. It means you aren't letting the loudest emotion lead the moment. Recognize the feeling and let it know you're going to put it on pause, just for a minute—just until your nervous system can take a breath.

Then we've learned to change the soundtrack, sometimes literally. Put on some calm music to change the vibe. Change your tone of voice. Slow down. When Chaos comes calling, one of the ways he'll pull you into his crazy is by trying to rush your words and your reactions. You start moving fast and mouthing off even faster. And none of that ever leads to anything good. So change your speed. Think before you talk.

Those emotions you sat in the corner for a minute? Now that you've got your breath back, and now that you've changed the soundtrack, invite those feelings back into the room. *Okay, this situation has me feeling some stress. And my heart is beating pretty fast. I'm feeling frustrated. What do I need in this moment to keep my calm amid the chaos? How about a quick prayer? Yes, that helps. Now, what is the first step I want to take here?* Talk to yourself, your emotions, and the emotions of your partner with kindness. Slowing down, taking some breaths, and observing the situation instead of getting sucked into it are all helpful ways to let Chaos know who's boss.

Yeah, Chaos is going to show up. But we don't have to let him move in. We sure don't need to feed him.

And Chaos doesn't get to convince us that our life isn't good.

We name this life, not him.

And we say it's good.

CHAPTER 7

FOCUS ON REFUSING TO AVOID YOUR PROBLEMS

One afternoon I (Sazan) sat fidgeting on the couch in my apartment. Kicking my foot back and forth. Running my sweaty hands over the legs of my jeans. Peeling my cuticles like it was my job.

I'd been living in LA for a couple of years by this point, and there was something I needed to do. Something I'd needed to do for a long time. But I knew it would be very hard and very scary. I knew what the likely outcome would be, and the pain of that had kept me from taking the next step.

But to get to what I knew God had for me, for my own good, it needed to happen.

I was so nervous that I took a moment to go back to my bedroom, saying I needed to go to the restroom. When I got to my room, my knees hit the floor. "Okay, God," I whispered. "You've got all of me. You've got to help me. Give me the words. You say go, and I'll do it. Help me." It wasn't the most eloquent prayer. But it was definitely heartfelt. After spending a few more minutes thinking and praying (and sweating), I got to my feet with God at my back. I opened the door to my bedroom and walked back out to the living room, perching again on the couch. A little more chitchat ensued. And then, it was time.

"Baba," I started, my voice a little shaky. "There's something I need to tell you."

Stevie's Side

Look, Sazan is a natural-born storyteller, and she's got a million of them. But let's back up here so I can fill you in on a couple of things. Several months before the day Sazan was just telling you about, we were in a place I call Stuck. Relationship-wise, that is. On the work front, I'd experienced a lot of rejection and heartache. And now, some exciting things were happening.

I'd just gotten a very cool contract to represent a food product I was really excited about. That job was going to take me on the road for five months. I'd be representing the product at different stops across the country. The timing was amazing; my roommate and I had been sleeping on air mattresses in our apartment, money so tight that I was living off frozen waffles and cheddar bratwursts and dreaming of the day I could afford a Chipotle burrito. It had been rough. Finally, with this new contract, the hustle and grind that had become a way of life after graduating from UNT seemed to be paying off.

But one little detail was making this time a mixed bag. While I couldn't wait to get going with this contract, I didn't really know where things stood with Sazan.

We'd been dating for a number of years, former college sweethearts now chasing our media dreams in LA. But from early on in our dating relationship, Sazan had always held back. She knew her family wouldn't accept our relationship, so she'd never told them about me. Fast-forward to now, and we'd been circling the *What Are We?* airport for a long time, with no plans to land on an answer in the foreseeable future.

Sazan was super excited and supportive of me taking on this contract. Which I appreciated. But her reaction was also kind of confusing. Would she miss me? Were we taking this thing between us, whatever it was, long-distance?

My attitude got . . . interesting. I didn't exactly friendzone Sazan, but I was acting pretty nonchalant about being gone for several months. I was giving off "well, we'll see" kinds of vibes. And I was doing a good job of convincing myself of that.

Did we even have the commitment and the chops to survive my drifting focus and the time apart?

Sazan Says

That's fair. I was really proud of Stevie for all his hard work and for getting this offer. But I didn't know where we stood either. As long as I wasn't ready to tell my family about him, we were in a holding pattern. It felt like a no-win situation. Get Stevie, lose my family. Keep my family, lose Stevie.

To be honest, I wasn't completely sure where Stevie stood in general. We were in a classic dating game of Texas Hold'em. I sure as heck wasn't going to wreck my family if the cards Stevie held didn't have a future with me in them. And I wasn't willing to show him my cards if I wasn't sure about his.

The day came when Stevie set out for this job. I didn't know how often I would get to see him, and I didn't know how often we would be in touch. What I did know was that as I told him goodbye, it felt like a real goodbye. Not a "see you later." His departure felt like a shift.

We'd been dancing around the same issues for years. Was this the relationship Stevie wanted for sure? What should I do about my family? We took what we'd been avoiding and just let the avoidance be the answer.

The answer seemed to be wrapped up in one gesture. A shrug.

"Are you and Stevie together?"

Shrug. "I don't know."

"When are you going to see each other again?"

Shrug. "I don't know."

"Do you have a future with Stevie?"

Pause. Shrug. "I don't know." *Ouch.*

So that's where we were: in the traffic circle of avoidance. We just kept going around and around. But when Stevie left on that trip, it felt like he'd exited into a new season of life. It wasn't that I didn't have my own stuff going on. My blog had taken off in ways I never could have imagined. We were each building unique careers—careers that made use of what we'd learned in our media training at college but that also took us in innovative directions.

But now, even though we'd had similar experiences amid the hustle of Los Angeles, the trajectories that had kept us in close orbit were starting to spin us out and away from each other. This also meant the issues we'd been avoiding were creating more and more distance the faster we spun into separate futures.

Stevie's Side

It's crazy to me, looking back, what happened once I hit the road for this job. Sazan and I only saw each other a handful of times. This was a big change from being together almost every day at college and cohosting the television show our department produced. Plus, once we both moved out to California, we were in each other's lives as often as we could be, usually several times a week. In between, we kept up a flurry of texts, phone calls, DMs, and cat memes.

Now, it was radio silence.

I tried not to think about it. And as you probably know, when you try not to think about something, you think about it all the time.

I wonder what Sazan . . . no, you idiot, don't think about her. Sazan, Sazan, Sazan . . .

But I was busy trying to do a good job for this company, busy being on the road, busy meeting people. And to be honest, I didn't know what I wanted with Sazan. Was I ready to settle down? What did "settling down" even mean? I hadn't dated much at all. Should I date more people, have more experiences, before making a lifelong commitment? Did I even want a serious relationship, or did I need more time to figure myself out?

Those are big questions, hard questions, and it felt easier to just leave them on the table than to gather them up and deal with them.

But God-led fate was coming for me. In the form of a movie rerun.

After just a few weeks into the contract, I was holed up in a hotel in Arizona. I had a rare night off and some time to myself. I turned on the television and started flipping through the channels, looking for a movie to watch to keep me company.

I found one that was familiar to me. I'd seen it a few times before, so it's not as if I didn't know the storyline or how the movie would end. I did. But I had no idea the impact it would make on me that night.

The movie was *Forrest Gump*, with Tom Hanks playing the lead character of Forrest and Robin Wright playing Jenny. In the film, Jenny and Forrest grow up together. Jenny's a spitfire. She takes care of Forrest and fights back the bullies who mock his kindness and his different way of expressing himself. As they age, life takes them toward different adventures and molds them in unique ways.

But one thing remains the same. Forrest loves Jenny. He calls her "my Jenny." Their lives meet and separate, meet and separate, over and over. But their love story is ultimately joined.

For a little while.

Then Jenny gets sick, and they only have a short amount of time as husband and wife before she dies. In one of the final scenes of the movie, Forrest stands over her grave, talking to her, telling her how the people they love are doing. He describes the latest happenings in their town, and how he had the childhood home where she was abused demolished.

He tells her again of his love and how he misses her.

My Jenny.

And your boy, Steve, alone in a hotel room in Arizona, just lost it.

Snot, tears, guttural cries.

I cried like a kid who's just broken his arm falling off his skateboard.

I cried like a toddler who's just busted his lip on the sidewalk.

I cried like a man who's suddenly realized he could lose one of the most precious things in his life.

Sazan was my Jenny. There it was, clear as day. I didn't want to spend the coming years running into her every now and then, never sure when we might meet again. I didn't want to stand over the grave of an unrealized relationship. I knew I'd never encounter another person in my life like Sazan, the Jenny to my Forrest.

I wanted to live my life *with* Sazan. I wanted us to have a life together. It was time to do the thing I'd been avoiding—putting all my cards on the table and taking the lead on this dance.

I'd love to tell you that I, with great panache and suaveness, made some killer move like driving through the night and arriving on Sazan's doorstep with an armload of flowers and a "You complete me" kind of Jerry Maguire speech on my lips.

But no.

Instead, this is how it went down. I finished watching *Forrest Gump*, bawled, and called Saz mid-bawl.

I'm my own kind of bawler, if you get the pun.

Through tears, I apologized to Sazan. I apologized for the way I'd been treating her, for making my career dreams bigger than our relationship. I apologized for becoming salty at God. I told her I wanted to stay together.

Then, I held my breath, waiting for her response.

The other end of the line was quiet. Until I heard her crying too. Then she told me she wanted this relationship. I didn't know how we would make this work. I didn't know what the timeline would look like or how we would navigate our issues.

What I did know was that I was going to ask this girl to marry me. I was going to save every bit of money I could while on the road, even if that meant going back to my exclusive ramen noodles diet. I was going to buy a ring and get down on one knee. It was my first step in running toward Sazan instead of galloping away from the challenges before us. Running toward, no longer running away.

Run, Stevie, run.

Sazan Says

That phone call was everything. It felt like, in a moment, we went from two people trying to figure out their stuff individually to one team.

We had *lots* to figure out. But now, we'd be making decisions as *us*, not as Stevie, the up-and-coming actor and television personality, and as Sazan, the beauty blogger and entertainment news correspondent.

That shift made the world different.

There was just one thing left that I needed to do. But it wasn't a little thing. And in our whole relationship, it was the thing I'd avoided the most: telling my family about this white boy who had my heart, the promise of the future I wanted.

You would think that Stevie's post–*Forrest Gump* revelation would have moved me into motion. But as big as my love for Stevie was (and is even bigger now every day), I still hesitated.

My parents still didn't know about a guy named Stephen Joshua Hendrix. In traditional Kurdish families, marriage is something that happens within the Kurdish community. You don't date outside your community. You don't marry outside your race.

When Stevie and I first started dating, I kept it hidden from my family and Kurdish friends. I figured there was no point in stirring up a hornet's nest of opinion if this thing with Stevie wasn't going to work out.

At least, that's what I told myself at the time.

It made for a pretty lopsided courtship. I got to know Stevie's family, his siblings, his buddies from high school. I had access to the world that had built him into the man he was. But on my side? He just had to take my word for it.

Our relationship kept growing, and I kept hiding. Hiding Stevie from my family. Hiding that I was undergoing this incredible experience of love. Hiding that my life might just take a different turn from what my Kurdish community and family hoped for me.

I kept putting it off.

After all, I didn't have any idea he was saving up for a ring. I didn't know when a proposal might be headed my way. And honestly, I didn't want to choose between my parents and Stevie. Why couldn't I have a romance like I'd seen other people have, where all the families were happy for the couple, where the land of family was something that grew to include loved ones instead of contracting to keep the original members inside the castle walls?

Stevie's Side

While out on the road, marking time and making money so I could get back to Sazan and we could start our lives together, I got another job offer.

Frankly, it was a dream job—one I should have accepted in a heartbeat.

So check this out.

Let's say you've been offered a job in an industry you'd always dreamed about. You would get to do many of the things you always hoped you would. You would also be meeting major industry movers and shakers, and your work would help shape conversations and trends in culture. And let's say this job offer came from someone whose star was rising crazy fast.

Oh, and it's likely that—eventually—you'd also get to sleep with your incredibly hot boss.

But that job offer?

You want to turn it down.

Welcome to a chapter from my life.

Hi, I'm Stevie Hendrix, and sometimes a dream job offer also comes with a chip on my shoulder.

That job offer was from Sazan. Her beauty blog and vlogs and collaborations suddenly went viral. I hate even to use the word *suddenly* because hard work, doubt, late nights, and early mornings had gone into everything she'd built before the numbers started to roll. But when all she'd been doing caught fire, so many things clicked into place. She was fielding more offers than she knew what to do with. She needed to produce content at a breakneck speed. She needed people to help manage what was now a full-fledged business, to help with media development, to help build the brand.

And she wanted me.

But what about *me*?

Sure, there was the *me* who knew how to do all those things, who believed in her and knew we could build this business as a team. But there was also this other version of *me*. The *me* who had told everyone back in the day that he was going to Hollywood. The *me* who had a vision of a standalone career—on camera, hosting, starring. The *me* who didn't want to ride on anyone's coattails.

That *me* was having a hard time. That *me* kept whispering things like, "Have some pride, man." And that *me* was not feeling too cooperative about Team Stevie and Sazan, LLC.

That *me* was close to messing things up for the other *me*.

If something's holding you back from fully seeing your good life, ask yourself: Does the good life look different from what you thought it would be? We resist what doesn't line up with how we envisioned it. But just because it looks different doesn't mean it's not good.

I called my dad, anxious to get some direction. I told him about my *Forrest Gump* revelation. I think I probably cried some more too. I told him about Sazan's idea of us working together. I told him about my fears surrounding the fact that she still hadn't talked to her family.

And as usual, Willie Hendrix showed up with the goods. He's the Yoda of What to Do Next. And why.

"Son, you're holding out," his voice rumbled down the phone line. "You've let her drive everything to this point. But she's at a place where she can't go any further until she knows what you're going to do. She needs to know you're committed. You can't ask her to tell her family about you, knowing that she stands every chance of being cut off from them. She needs you in her court. In love, in business, in life."

I went back through all my Hollywood dreams. Was I going to walk away from this? Did loving Sazan mean letting go of what I'd been working toward all this time?

"You can do whatever you want, son. I think working on all these projects together *could* be a realization of your dreams. But if you're not all in, she needs to know. You need to tell her."

"It just seems so risky," I replied. "I mean, she hasn't even told her parents about us yet, and now we're talking about me walking away from the inroads I've made in LA to work with her. I could get shredded on this thing."

"Yeah, you could." *Gee, thanks for the pep talk, Pop.* "But you'll never know if you don't lead on this. She'll tell her folks when she knows where you stand. Tell her."

Sazan Says

We sat in Stevie's car after he got back to town for good. He'd accepted my job offer. We were working together. We were planning a life together. We were a team.

I wish I could tell you that, so powerful was my love for Stevie, so swept away by his declaration of love and commitment, I immediately sat my parents down and told them, steel in my spine, about my forbidden romance.

But that wouldn't be the truth.

In reality, Stevie knew I would have to work up to it. So we set a deadline for Thanksgiving, which was three months away. I'd tell them after Thanksgiving dinner, when I went to visit them in Dallas. I'd sit them down, explain that I was in love with a white boy from Austin, and they'd have to accept it or accept the consequences, dang it.

Three months. I could do it. I rehearsed my lines and rehearsed all the outcomes. I worked up my courage and calmed my nerves.

Thanksgiving came.

And went.

I know, I know. I can't tell you the number of times I tried to get the words out. But there's no easy way to break your parents' hearts. And I knew that's what this would do. I sat at that Thanksgiving table and thought, *Who am I kidding? I can't do this right now.*

I was so disappointed in myself for not doing what I'd been avoiding. After all, Stevie and I had come up with a plan. Stevie had declared himself and had started working with me. Now, it was my turn.

God and I had several conversations following my failure to launch at Thanksgiving. *God, this is yours. When you know it's the right time, I need you to give me a nudge,* I prayed. *I can't do this without you. I need a sign.*

A couple of weeks after Thanksgiving, my dad came to see me in Los Angeles. One afternoon, my sister was out for the day, and my dad and I had time to ourselves at my apartment. When he arrived and I let him in the door, I felt it. *The nudge.* We sat on the couch. It would have looked like a casual chat to anyone who walked in the room, and that's what my dad thought it was. But I was practically vibrating with nervous energy and the loud debate that was taking place in my head.

It was such a clear moment to tell him. But once again, I was tongue-tied.

That's when I excused myself for a moment. Hit my knees in a frantic prayer. Asked God to give me a sign, to push me. Then headed back out to the living room.

I took a seat across from my dad. He picked up our conversation again. "So what I was thinking, Sazan, is this. You and your siblings, none of you are married or dating. Your mother and I could buy property, probably in Texas. And I could build a house where all five of you could live together. That way, we could always have a life together. We could all be together on the same land."

"No," I responded. "No, Baba, there's something I need to tell you." It was time to jump.

This was my opening—my sign from God.

"Baba, that's not the life for me. It's sweet of you to offer to do something like that, but no. I want a different life for myself. As a matter of fact, I'm in love with a white boy. Stevie. I'm going to marry him, and we're going to build a life together. That's the life I want."

And what followed was . . . silence.

Absolute silence.

My dad sat there on the couch. He looked at me for a few moments. Then he looked across the room. Then at his hands.

Soon, he pulled out his phone and started scrolling. Awhile later, a phone call came through from a family member. He answered. "Hello! Yes, yes, how are you? Yes, I'm just here visiting with Sazan . . ." He stood and continued chatting, taking the rest of the call on the small porch outside. When he came back in, he returned to silence.

After several long hours, I couldn't take it anymore. "Baba, are you going to say anything?!" I asked.

He sighed. "Sazan, you know where I stand on this. Your mother and I have only asked one thing of you: that you would follow our guidance and let us help you find someone Kurdish to marry. You know what this means." And then he left.

Was I sad? Of course. Did I understand my dad's reaction? Yes. Being Kurdish is fundamental to my family, and I was stepping outside of what was seen as supportive of that. Did my heart ache? Absolutely.

Was there also a sense of relief?

One thousand percent.

A couple of weeks later, Stevie proposed.

I answered with a clear heart. No more hiding, only truth.

Yes.

We're all avoiding something. Sometimes it's the small things, like cleaning out that drawer you can barely close. Sometimes it's things that could help move your business along, like finishing your website.

Sometimes, it's committing to a decision you know will hold both good and hard.

Call it procrastination. Call it timing. Call it whatever.

But the longer you take to call it, the more it costs you.

The longer you and I hold off from doing the hard thing, the longer we hold off from getting to the good. The hard is the way to the good. And believe me, I'm all about looking for God's timing and not getting ahead of him.

But I also know I can miss God's timing when I keep holding out.

I don't know what you're holding out on, but I bet you have something. A chore you don't feel like doing. A hard conversation you don't want to have. You've got plenty of reasons. They're probably really good ones.

> # The hard is the way to the good.

But a good excuse can't replace your one beautiful, good life.

Stevie and I have learned the long way. Which is often the hard way.

Doing the hardest thing is a good thing. You can't outwait God's invitation to take a step into your future. That step often comes with a steep cost. And if you've decided something is worth it—really worth it—take the step. Do the thing you've been avoiding.

Sometimes it's the only thing standing between you and what God has for you.

CHAPTER 8

FOCUS ON GOODNESS IN HOPELESS MOMENTS

M y (Sazan's) mom's car had broken down again. It happened so often that my five-year-old self assumed cars were supposed to break down as much as they worked. I'm sure it caused a lot of inconvenience for my parents, but for me, it meant my mom would walk me to school. The school wasn't very close, probably thirty minutes one way. My short legs didn't help the situation. During our slow walks, I'd point out bugs and flowers and puppies while my mom nodded sweetly the way parents do with their kids.

If you've ever gone on a long walk with a small child, you know getting somewhere on time is a complicated production. But since we were going to school, Mom didn't want me to be late. Her solution? About halfway through the walk, she would swoop me up on her shoulders to pick up the pace. I don't know why this was so much fun, but it was! I loved seeing the world from so high up. I would wrap my arms around her forehead and reach out for tree limbs overhanging the sidewalk.

Close to the school, there was a short back road full of fruit trees. Apples, peaches, figs, pears. A grapevine with massive leaves as big as my head. It was like a natural produce section in the grocery store. Whenever I was on Mom's shoulders, she would detour through the produce aisle. I think she planned it because she would always reach into her pocket, bring out a small bag, and hand it to me as she got close to the trees. That was my cue. Once she was under the canopy, I'd inspect different fruits and pluck them from the branches. Mom would give the final approval, and I would slip them into the bag. It felt like a little scavenger hunt. Looking back, it was so much more.

These walks to school were our time together, our chance to enjoy each other despite whatever hardships we were facing as a family. I was my mom's little helper, and that made me so happy. It also showed me that my mom wanted to be with me, to amble along the side road toward the delight of letting me pick the fruit. We probably wouldn't do this for more than five minutes—I still had to get to school. I'm sure she had plenty to do too. But that five-minute detour left a mark on my heart that only a loving mom can leave.

Now that I'm a mom, I see how a lot more went on with those walks than I realized as a kid. I've gotta be honest; if I had to walk Teeny to preschool for thirty minutes one way, walk back home for thirty minutes, and then do it all over again the next day—and do it often—I'd be struggling.

My mom had plenty on her plate to deal with during the day. These side excursions had to have undone her schedule. That detour to pick some fruit, I now can see, was also a necessity with our tiny grocery budget.

Think about how your day gets completely off track. Your plan gets sidelined. The flight is delayed, then delayed again, then canceled. The subway line is closed for maintenance. The car you just got out of the shop goes down with the same issue again. What words come to mind?

Frustrated.
Inconvenienced.
Stressed.
Mad.

Those are all legitimate feelings in those kinds of situations. But choosing to live a good life, choosing to make this one day a good day, also means choosing a different way of looking at things. It means *making* good in the midst of experiencing the inconvenient, the frustrating, the bad.

That's what my mom was doing. She was creating good memories and good times and good connection amid aggravation and disruption. And what I got to have as a result were some of the sweetest moments between a mom and a daughter. That broken-down car was the un-intended invitation into these moments. When my mom's car worked, we didn't walk to school. That junkie old car caused a lot of heartache for my parents, but it also provided a hidden blessing—and lots of fruit. Those walks taught me that adversity can open new, surprising, wonderful moments of connection, joy, and love.

·   ·   ·

The ways we want to get somewhere don't always work.

Maybe you went on that dating app all of your friends were on. They all found "The Dude," but you've only met a series of duds. Maybe you did all the things you were supposed to do to fast-track your career, but it's fallen flat.

You've tried all the hacks to beat the algorithm, you've connected with all the right people, you've gone to the right places and been in the right rooms. You're doing all the things everyone said will get you where you want to go. But for some reason, you still find yourself having to walk to school.

So now what?

It can feel hopeless.

And it can feel like you must be doing something wrong since everyone else seems to get different, better results, doing the same things you're doing.

I'm all for checking my form, if you will, and making sure I'm not accidentally sabotaging myself when I'm not getting the results I'd hoped. Having accountability with Stevie, checking in with mentors I trust—these steps can help me get on track if I've lost my way. But I'm here to tell you that sometimes, that's just the way it goes. The formulas that have carried other people to success just don't work the same way for me. What's up with that?

When I sit with people who've lived some life, people who've lived through some serious stuff, I find something important. Though these people have lived good lives, not everything in their lives has been good. They are the people who know how to search out, create, and experience good when the going gets tough.

Just like my mom did with her broken-down car, they view the "rogue times" as an invitation. An opportunity.

I promise you, making good in the midst of bad is a sign of maturity. And to be honest, I don't want to be a grown-up some days. I want to throw the tantrum, insisting that it needs to work out the way I want it to. I stomp around and punch my fists down by my sides.

"It's not fair," I chant, as if my words will change anything. "It's not fair."

And it's not. But *fairness* doesn't really have much to do with living a good life. There's a scripture in the Bible where Jesus says that God "causes his sun to rise on the evil and the good, and sends rain on the righteous and the unrighteous" (Matthew 5:45). Jesus is talking to a group of people whose lives depend on the weather and how it affects their crops.

> They are the people who know how to search out, create, and experience good when the going gets tough.

And he's reminding them that *because* God is a loving God, life won't seem fair at times. The farmer next door might be a complete jerk, but he's going to have sunshine and rain on his crops, just as you do on yours. His wheat might even grow a little higher.

His car might be more dependable, if you know what I mean.

Jesus wraps what he's saying in a reminder to not only love those who are easy to love, but to love those who feel like enemies. It's an invitation to find goodness, and to respond with goodness, even when conditions aren't fair, even when things seem a little hopeless.

It's looking for the fruit when the car is dead.

It's taking a better path.

. . .

My dad had just opened a new restaurant in Irving, Texas, about forty-five minutes from our house. On the days my mom's car was on the outs, he would leave Barzan's Café, pick up my mom, and pick up my sisters and me from school. When we all loaded in, the car was cramped, just like our apartment!

To be blunt, we were poor and lived in a tiny apartment. When I say *tiny*, I mean it. As I mentioned before, there were two bedrooms and a third "bedroom," which was a converted laundry room. Eight of us were living there, so no one had any privacy. That cramped apartment helped us forge a remarkable bond as a family—one that was tested but remained powerful as my siblings and I headed into adulthood.

One day, when we got back home, I raced up the flight of stairs ahead of everyone else. It wasn't long after Christmas. My parents had scraped and saved for what we considered the ultimate Christmas present: a new Nintendo gaming system. After getting home from school that day, I wanted to be first to grab a controller. (Also, I know I'm dating myself with the Nintendo. Trust me, back then, Nintendo was *everything*.)

When I got to the front door, though, it was already open. *That's odd*, I thought. Then other details came into focus. The wood frame surrounding the deadbolt was splintered and cracked.

"We've been robbed!" I yelled down the stairs. I didn't really know what I was talking about. I only said that because I'd seen it in a cartoon and was just being silly.

Well, it turned out I was right. As the rest of my family came to the door, my dad peeked in and saw everything tossed, scattered, and messy. We all stayed outside, and my parents called the police. Within fifteen minutes, two squad cars pulled up with their flashing lights. We heard their sirens in the distance, and the street felt so quiet once they turned them off. They came to our apartment with their game faces on. They didn't so much as say hello as they pulled out their firearms and entered. Because our place was so small, it didn't take them long to do a full sweep. All they really had to do was stand in the middle of the room and rotate in a circle.

They soon came out and assured us the apartment was empty and that it was safe to go in. My mom, sisters, and I all went to the bedrooms to assess the damage while my dad gave the police some details about our home and belongings.

The police were courteous and promised to do their best to find the thief, but we all knew deep down that the person responsible, and our stolen possessions, would never be found. We would be left with the loss with no explanation or justice. We didn't have much to steal; I mean, seriously, if the robber had just *asked* if our aparmtnet was worth breaking into, I would have told him straight up it wasn't worth the time.

Once the police left and we had taken stock, we all gathered in the living room to list what we knew had been taken. Sure enough, the Nintendo was gone. My sisters and I started bawling about it. We knew my parents didn't have the money to replace it, and it made me feel angry and icky to think about Mario collecting coins with someone else's fingers on *my* controller. The TV was gone, too, so no more cartoons. The robber even raided our freezer and took our meat. It still strikes me as so random. Meat. Our frozen meat was taken. It reminds me of the scene in *How the Grinch Stole Christmas* when the Grinch takes the last crumb from a mouse.

Every crumb that mattered to us was gone.

The saddest loss of all was a small collection of watches my dad owned. They weren't flashy or expensive, but he displayed and took care of them like they were Hublots, Rolexes, and Movados. He had saved for them, and they were mementos of his hard work and dedication.

Whatever little we had, we now had less of it.

As we all sat together, a heavy silence filled the room. My sisters and I didn't know what to say and had no idea what my parents would do. Would Baba fume? Would Mom cry? We waited for them to react so we would know how we should feel too.

What happened next has stuck with me my whole life. Mom and Baba got up and gathered us in their arms. They said, "What matters most is that we still have each other, and we won't let anyone ever take

101

that away." Their faces were full of comfort and gratitude as they looked each of us in the eyes and squeezed us tight.

They chose to look for goodness in a hopeless moment.

I'd love to tell you that their example immediately took hold of my heart and changed the trajectory of my frantic thoughts. In the moment, it did help me regain some sense of safety, but if I'm being honest, that feeling of safety was brief. Starting that day and for many days after, I felt a foreboding sense of fear and violation in our house. *What if the robber comes back? What if they take me this time?* I kept imagining someone else's hands in my dresser drawer and thinking about how their greedy eyes had scanned everything I owned. I had a hard time going into my room by myself, and I'd make one of my sisters go in with me at bedtime.

Starting the night of the break-in, I prayed to God that we would never get robbed again.

And just like that, the brokenness of that violation grafted onto my heart.

That's probably not what you expected me to say—that after praying that prayer, I felt more violated and scared than ever. But here's the deal. What I was asking for was to never have to experience those kinds of emotions again. To never feel taken advantage of. To never again feel the unfairness of such a violation. The prayer I prayed was not a prayer that would loosen the grip of fear.

But there was a prayer out there that could have actually given me freedom instead of a lingering dread. And that prayer was for God to set me free from fear, despite the circumstances coming my way. Such a prayer asked for the ability to see beauty and strength and goodness in any situation.

That freedom didn't happen overnight, but it's something God has taught me over time.

God exchanged my ideas about fairness with the freedom from fear.

When I think about my mom on our walks to school or about my parents after we got robbed, I now see how those moments helped me understand more of who God is. In some way, the hardship we faced as a family enabled God to show me more of his heart *for me*. It makes me tear up to think this is how God works—that the stuff I'd rather avoid becomes the raw material he remakes into expressions of his love and character. The world will try to tell you that a hopeless situation only has that in it: hopelessness. But I'm here to tell you, because I've seen it again and again, there is good amid hopelessness. You may have to dig to find it. You might only see it after many tears and a lot of questions. But it's there, waiting for you.

Maybe something in your life feels broken right now. Maybe a dream you've held for a long time has hit the rocks. Or your heart is tossed in the wake of a difficult breakup. Maybe you've broken promises to yourself, and you don't know how to get back to a better place. I get it. I've lived through a lot of brokenness.

When builders get ready to build a new building, what do they do? They break up the ground of the build site to prepare it. When a farmer gets ready to plant a new crop, he breaks up the soil so a new crop can grow. There have been so many times in my life that God has taken the pieces of my broken heart, my broken dreams, or my broken resolve and used them to do something new in my life. He's taken what I thought was pulverized and used it as the pulp to create new pages in the story of my life.

> I'm here to tell you, there is good amid hopelessness.

And I believe he'll do it for you, too, when you lay all the fragments of your patchwork heart in his gentle hands. God sacrificed the life of his one and only son so that we could have a better life—a life with God as a loving, caring Father. And that's something no one can take away.

What if? What if you declared the shards you're standing on to be new ground? What if you asked God to do something with the pieces of what you can't hold together anymore? What if you asked him to create something better out of your loss? If you open your heart to what brokenness can bring, you may find blessings and memories and love. Broken isn't always bad. Broken things can grow back stronger when we let them.

Even when it feels like you have to take the long way around. Even when you have to go out of your way.

Growing back stronger is good.

EVENING
GATHER

Our daily time to gather is when the daylight begins to fade each evening, when Sazan and the girls and I meet in the kitchen to prep dinner after the work projects are done for the day. Amari shows us her latest dance moves and chomps on blackberries. Teeny tells us about her new friend at school. We talk about the events of the day. Butter and onions sizzle in the sauté pan, and Sazan shows the girls how to lay out the silverware. It's simple.

It's profound.

Whom you gather with and how you prioritize gathering tells you a lot about your life. We can claim that this or that friendship is super important. We can say our faith is the central point in our life. We can declare that family comes first. But all that's just talk if we don't take the time to gather with those people and that faith community.

Some of my happiest, good-life moments have happened when gathering with the people I love. Some of my toughest moments have been when I've isolated myself or let other ambitions and tasks replace the discipline of gathering.

Yeah, I said it. Gathering is a discipline.

Many things will try to pull you away from gathering with your people. Busy schedules. Hurt feelings. Getting lost in your phone. Or getting lost in your priorities. But I'm convinced that each day needs a time for gathering. Each good life is marked by circling up with your people.

Yes, I'm all for the holiday celebrations and the birthday parties. That's prime gathering real estate. But don't miss out on the small and the simple.

And the daily. I don't want to sleep through this one good day. I want to be awake and alert, circled up around the kitchen island. I'm reminding myself of this. And I'm reminding you.

This day, this evening, take some time to huddle up. With that friend you've been meaning to see. With that family member who needs a listening ear. With that neighbor who's been asking to go for a walk.

Yes, the evening is here. And time for rest will come. But for now, right now, gather. Gather those you love in hugs. Gather smile lines at the corners of your eyes. Gather stories.

Gather together.

Because each day, even a random Tuesday evening over mac and cheese, is a celebration. And family is built one gathering at a time.

CHAPTER 9

FIND YOUR PEOPLE AND GATHER

One evening I (Sazan) thought, *Maybe it's us. Maybe we're the problem.*

Stevie and I love being part of a community. Love it. We love hosting dinner parties and game nights. We love hearing people's stories until the wee hours of the morning. We love helping people move into their new houses. We love having adventures and experiences with people.

For us, our community is an extension of our family. We need people around us who don't take life too seriously but are serious about friendship and doing life together.

While we were still living in Los Angeles after getting married in 2015, we had our people. Boy, did we have our people. We called our group the LA Familia. We were a group of people in different seasons of life. Some in the group were still single or single again. Some were younger and some were older. Some were also in the entertainment industry, and some weren't.

We'd found each other in a variety of ways, but what I mainly remember was how simple it felt.

We were an extended family.

We all lived in close proximity to each other, which meant we were able to be part of each other's daily lives. I know you can have incredible friendships with people who live halfway across the country. I have those kinds of friendships, too, and they are precious and important.

But there's something about dashing in and out of each other's houses, popping by on a random Tuesday evening, or stopping by with the gallon of milk your friend needed from the store that has an incredible sweetness to it.

That's how we lived.

Familia.

When we began a house hunt in 2017, we wanted more than anything to stay in the area of Los Angeles where we currently lived—because of LA Familia. But while our prayers were answered for a home we were absolutely crazy about, it was miles and miles from the community we'd developed. Which sucked.

All that ease of being together disappeared. Gathering took planning. It took more time. And while that community was worth it, the natural time constraints and distance did their thing. As did life. People who were part of our group of friends also started moving, some of them across the country. Others got new jobs south of Los Angeles or farther north. Over time, that special season of living the LA Familia life came to a close.

It was a bummer.

And it left Stevie and me longing to develop a new community. *We've got this*, we thought. *We're friendly people. We know how to make friends, right?* But it did not come easily.

I think we can probably agree that making friends as adults is kind of weird. Not that friendships in school were all that simple, but think about it: In elementary school, you were assigned a desk. And whether you wanted to or not, you probably got to know the people sitting in your part of the classroom. You might wave at one of your desk buddies in the cafeteria line. And by fall break, just because you were together every day, doing the same assignments, having the same recess, you at least had a pool of people to pick from for friendship.

Same for high school.

Same for college.

Then adulthood comes along. And unless you've got some kind of situation like *The Office* going on, it can get awkward.

Heck, even on *Friends*, the odds of friendship are better than a usual situation. Monica and Ross are siblings. Chandler was Ross's roommate in college, so Monica, Ross, and Chandler already know each other. When Chandler and Joey move in across the hall from Monica's apartment, she already knows Chandler, and Joey gets pulled into the group. Rachel and Monica went to school together from elementary days on up, so Rachel already knows Ross too. Phoebe is the only true outlier of the group.

So, yeah, figuring out how to find your people when you've got a job and #adulting responsibilities is new territory.

You'd think that with all the people we routinely interacted with through our brand platforms, a group would begin to emerge. We were also going on these incredible trips with other influencers, having Instagram-worthy adventures with people close to our own age and in similar seasons of life.

But you know and I know that Instagram isn't always real life. As in, hardly ever real life. All the friendly banter and cute photos and #ilysm and #besties tags didn't have staying power in our actual lives.

After a bit of frustration on that front, we had ourselves a little conference, Stevie and me. *We need to dig in more at church*, we said. *We need to do more than just showing up for services. We'll sign up for stuff, and we'll reach out and find community there. Go Team Hendrix Friend Search!*

So that was us. Signing up for all the things. Going to the young married classes and socials. Being friendly and reaching out. *Hey! Over here! Let's be friends, mkay?!*

But nothing seemed to be clicking. People were perfectly nice.

But they didn't feel like *our* people.

Were we too picky? It didn't feel like it. Were we too weird and zany? That might track. But we'd found weird, zany people before, people we absolutely vibed with. If we were going to have community, true community, then the people who made up that community would definitely need to be okay with my impromptu dance parties and Stevie's odd collection of voices and accents he uses on the reg.

Right?

I've got to pause here and tell you something so important about finding your people. You may feel like you're supposed to be friends with some people simply because they're the popular ones. They're going to the cool places and getting the awesome opportunities. Or they seem to be in the clique everyone wants to be in. They're leading the ministry team at church. Or they're the group that goes to lunch every day from the office. They have a bond, and they've got chemistry.

They're the *shiny people*.

And you want to be *shiny people* too.

Honestly? Stevie and I have dealt with this. We pursued friendships with people because they were shiny, and we hoped some of that shine would rub off on us. I didn't think that's what we were doing at the time, but as I look back, I can see it. And because Stevie and I live so much of our lives online, some people out there may think of *us* as the shiny people, even though we try to show up in all the versions of ourselves, including the goofy, gassy ones.

Let's face it. We probably all have those people whose lives we think of as perfect and fascinating and successful, though we have no idea of what really goes down at home. Those people.

But lean in here: *They may not be your people.* Because your people have special skills. Your people might not be the ones everyone notices at first.

Your people? They are the people . . .

- who love to make you laugh until you snort.
- who keep old-school Pringles (or better yet, Flamin' Hot Cheetos) in the pantry for when you come over.
- whom you can call in the middle of the night when a water pipe bursts.

When you're lonely for community, one of the bigger, easiest-to-make mistakes is to look for a community you want to be like and hope to get grandfathered in. Understandably, you don't want to start from scratch—but you might not be all that honest with yourself about who you are and who you really jell with.

It takes courage to let go of drifting toward the "popular kids." Instead, take a risk and invest in a friend group that really gets you.

So there we were. While we still hadn't found a community like we'd had, we were thankful to still be doing a lot of life with the couple who were our best friends.

That is, until they let us in on a little life change.

They were moving.

Another one bites the dust.

We were excited for them, but we knew things would change. Of course we would remain close.

But they moved away. And we were back to a pretty solitary life.

Holed up in our new house. Me hugely pregnant with Valentina. The remaining LA Familia over a forty-minute drive away. Going to a nice, new church, but struggling to get plugged in.

We were back where we started. Stevie and I wondered if we were the problem—if we had lost our friendship mojo. We felt really isolated, and we'd burned through all the ways we could think of to find our people.

I was spending more and more time at the house, working a lot, and spending a lot of time online. Alone.

That's when I spotted something.

A YouTube thumbnail popped up on my suggestions page with an image of a gorgeous wedding. I just had to click it. It was a vlog of a girl, Kristin Johns, and her husband, Marcus. They were hilarious. They loved Jesus. They enjoyed great design and travel. They took amazing pictures.

So I did what anyone in that situation would do.

I started stalking her.

Okay, now, hold on. Before you get all freaked out, just know I healthy stalked her. I watched all her YouTube vlogs. I started following her on Instagram.

You know, not creepy stalking. Just a little light stalking.

Decorative stalking.

Something about her resonated with me. She seemed like my kind of people—down-to-earth and kind. She was silly. She was creative. She also had a golden retriever, just like me.

Then I did something weird.

You probably already know what I'm going to say. *No, you didn't.*

Oh, yes. I did.

I slid into her DMs.

There, I said it. I slid in Kristin Johns's DMs. Like a proper stalker.

I figured my message would eventually meet the delete button. But Kristin messaged me back! She had checked out who I was, and in fact, she had started following me three days earlier by recommendation of her sister-in-law. We started chatting back and forth through our DMs.

She lived fifteen minutes away from me. Check. She was also making her way through the ups, downs, and sideways of making a living online. Check. She valued her relationship with God. Check. Her marriage was a priority. Check.

We took a chance on each other and set up a playdate for our dogs.

Yep. The first time we met in person was to get our golden retrievers together at her home.

Our friendship blossomed. We got our husbands together, and they hit it off as well. (It's a funny story because Stevie had a dream that he and Marcus were hanging out a couple of years before they actually met. Definitely God working!) That friendship carried us and fed us. Sure, our community was smaller now. But Kristin and Marcus became our community, our family. We lived far away from our relatives, but finding your people gives you a home. Finding your people helps the good in your life to flourish.

Am I telling you to research the Instagram influencers in your neighborhood and try to forge a friendship through their DMs? Um, no, I am not.

What I am saying is that it might take some work to find your people. You might have to go about it in ways that feel a little uncomfortable. You have to put yourself out there.

If you've been fortunate enough to have experienced a powerful community in your life, you know how transformative it can be. Stevie and I struggled after leaving the LA Familia because we wanted to replicate that wonderful experience exactly. We longed for the days when LA Familia members were in and out of each other's daily lives all the time. We longed for the same incredible connection with new friends.

Guess what? It's okay for what you need in community and for the rhythms of that community life to change.

In our time of building a relationship with Kristin and Marcus, we learned that community can look many different ways at different times in your life. Really, after Teeny was born, Stevie and I could see that even if we'd stayed closer to the LA Familia group, things would have changed anyway after her birth. Because our entire lives were changing.

Look, change will come to your community. It doesn't mean something's wrong. That's just how life turns and shifts. It doesn't mean the friendships failed somehow. It doesn't mean it's wrong to take the new job in the next city. It doesn't mean you shouldn't love with your whole heart the people you're doing life with right now.

What matters most is embracing the community you have today. And if you're in the weird in-between of having wrapped up a season in a community you've loved, it's okay. I'm learning that different seasons of life—such as stages of parenting or decisions Stevie and I make about where we're going to live—all impact what we need out of community and what we have to give. It's all good.

I wish I had some magic formula to share for finding your people. Really, at the end of the day, you can only prioritize the search. You have to be willing to put yourself out there and be awkward if needed. It's about taking a chance.

.   .   .

Stevie and I are again in a season of rebuilding community. When we moved back to Texas, we were in the middle of a little thing called a pandemic (hello, 2020!). And as it turns out, launching into the waters of Making New Friends is hard when you're in lockdown. Having a newborn during lockdown doesn't make it easier. Only recently have we been able to come up for air.

But I can tell you this. Whether we're in a season of rich community or whether we're feeling the drought, people are central to living the good life. You don't need many, but you need quality. You need people who sharpen you, love you, track with you, challenge you, gather with you, and grow with you.

Think outside of the box. Stop running toward the cool kids. There are people out there who are looking for you, just like you are looking for them. Say some prayers along the way that God will connect you to those you can walk through life with.

Here's an idea: Who can you think of, right now, who is a quiet person in your life? Someone who's pretty reserved in the office, or who doesn't speak up too much at your church small group? Make it a point to chat with that person this week. Find out where they are from. Ask if they're a dog or a cat person (and then don't judge them for their answer). I can already hear your thoughts: *I don't know how comfortable I am doing that. That seems pretty forward. What if they think I'm a weirdo?*

Look, all relationships take risk. Sure, somebody might not understand why you're suddenly chatting them up. But if you're waiting for someone to come along and sweep you into a friendship circle, you could be waiting a good long while.

> **You need people who sharpen you, love you, track with you, challenge you, gather with you, and grow with you.**

Friendships take courage. Connections take conversations. Challenge yourself to meet one new person a week. And by new person, I don't necessarily mean someone you've never encountered before. Like I said, it could be an individual who's been in the background of your life.

Stevie and I are also big believers in setting a time and place to consistently be with friends. When we were in LA, we routinely had "family dinners" with our community. We celebrated birthdays and promotions. We put those dates on the calendar in ink and honored them. We hosted often. Again, you've got to invest in community, and the lifeblood of community is being present. Look for regular times to meet, to break bread, to do life. Make it simple by making, say, the third Thursday night of every month your community time. Start a supper club to test your recipes out. Start a book club that meets every four weeks. (Hey, you could even make this book the first one you read together!)

Don't forget about the people who literally live around you. So many of us have no idea who our neighbors are anymore, yet those are often the people it would be the easiest to build community with. If your neighborhood or apartment complex doesn't have one yet, start a Facebook page or some sort of place to gather online where you can look out for one another. Stop to chat with people you encounter on your walks.

> **A good life is seasoned with good friends. Relationships bring spice to your life and sweetness to your days.**

If all of this makes you feel flooded with social anxiety, I get it. Putting yourself out there can be hard. But remember that you were built for community. You're doing something good for yourself when you step out there. You're on a treasure hunt, and you don't want to miss the gold.

A good life is seasoned with good friends. Relationships bring spice to your life and sweetness to your days. Dr. Mark Hyman says it this way: "The power of community to create health is far greater than any physician, clinic or hospital."[1]

I want that kind of health for me, even in this season of starting over. And I want it for you.

CHAPTER 10

DISCONNECT TO CONNECT AND GATHER

O ne evening, I found Stevie in tears.

Which, as you know, is one of the things I love about my man. He's got all the feels.

"Babe," I asked, "what's going on? Why the tears?"

He'd been scrolling through a bunch of video footage on his phone and came across videos of Teeny when she was . . . teenier. A baby. Tiny. And it really got him going—how fast time is flying, how fast she's growing.

He told me, "I remember this time, her being so little. But I feel like so much was going on then, going through my mind. I was so over-whelmed that I wanted to escape. I wasn't content. I was being selfish, wanting to do what I want to do instead of being grounded. I loved her like crazy, but I was trying to figure out the whole fatherhood thing while still being consumed with the LA grind."

He took a deep breath before continuing. "Where did the time go, and why was I rushing it? I was too connected to my own inner dialogue and ambitions to face the beautiful reality right in front of me!"

First of all, is anything more handsome or compelling than a guy who owns his emotions, admits his mistakes, cries over videos of his baby girl, and has incredible honesty and insight? No. No, there is not. Dassa *man* right there. My man.

He told me he was glad we had moved away from Los Angeles. He felt like he would have missed our kids growing up. No disrespect to LA. We loved our time there. But it's so easy when you're plugged into the competitiveness and hustle of that city to lose track of yourself.

He couldn't believe he'd let that time pass by so quickly.

Here's the good part, the part that came out of that hard insight: When Amari was born, he made good on what he'd realized. Instead of getting all up in his head, he was determined to embrace both the good and the hard that comes with having a newborn in the house. When Amari was a couple of months old, she had terrible indigestion. She was the sweetest baby, but when her tummy would get going, she would just wail.

The one place she wanted to be?

On Stevie's chest.

So many evenings, she'd get cranked up and I'd be at the point of total meltdown. We would bounce. We would rock. We would feed. Still, her tummy would cramp.

Stevie would take her and get her nestled on his chest, her tummy against him, and she'd calm down. She'd snuggle in. She'd sleep.

Which meant I got to catch up on some sleep too.

And Stevie? He drank it in. He was present. He disconnected from everything else and paid attention to the treasure snoozing on his chest. He gathered up that little baby and was just *with her*.

It's one thing to figure out you've missed some important chunks of your life. It's a whole other thing to make it different moving forward.

. . .

Have you ever thought about all the things you're connected to?

Sure, you have a phone and screens that seem to be everywhere.

But you're also connected to a friend group.

Your job.

Your church.

Your neighborhood.

Your city.

Your schedule.

Your extended family.

Your thought patterns.

The past.

The future.

The way it's "supposed to be."

I don't think I realized how many things I was connected to that were pulling me away from the moment. All those connections just kind of happened. Another opportunity or distraction or request would come my way, and I'd grow another cable, tethering myself to yet one more obligation. Or one more event. Or one more negative thought.

That's the thing with all those connections. They're like wires coming out of your head and heart, sprouting in all different directions.

And they can get tangled up so fast.

. . .

We moved to Austin right before the pandemic began. Our new home required a lot of upgrades, so while the renovation was underway, we lived with Stevie's mom and dad. There we all were, locked down together, waiting out a pandemic. It was a lot of people and a lot of togetherness. Which was sweet in a lot of ways.

And also stressful.

It happened so casually that I didn't think much about it at first. But every day, Teeny would escape to a closet at my in-laws' house. She'd claimed it as her own little spot. It wasn't a huge closet, and it didn't have any cool closet features. But it was big enough for a little girl with a big imagination to make a place of her own among a houseful of people.

She moved a few toys in there. Some books. Some treasures and odds and ends.

After she set it up, she began inviting guests.

"Mommy," she'd ask me at various times throughout the day, "would you like to come to my house?"

You know, I'd love to tell you my answer was a no-brainer, that I'd stop whatever I was doing and head in there with her. But I was connected to so much in the moment that getting all those "wires" off would take some time.

Once I entered Teeny's closet, though, and once I started doing it every day, the magic happened.

We'd go in that little closet, and a whole new world would open up. We'd dream up stories. We'd line up her little figurines and come up with dialogue. We'd create art together. New songs. Silly jokes. Dramas.

Joy.

Teeny's closet was our own little playland. Whatever was happening on the other side of that closet door didn't matter once I entered her world. We would reconnect. It was liberating.

She started inviting other family members to join her at her "house," so we all began to experience the same thing. A sense of escape from a world gone wild. A few minutes to take a breath and focus on this imaginative toddler. A chance to set everything else aside. A handful of moments in a little secret garden of Teeny's invention. It felt like the most real part of my day.

When we disconnected from the pressure and calls and worry, we could connect with Valentina. Connect with ourselves. Connect with some peace.

That's when I started to figure it out. You've got to disconnect to connect.

.   .   .

At certain times in my life, I've become unconsciously connected to a whole lot. Of course, whenever I think about disconnecting and connecting, my phone, my laptop, and all my screens come to mind. When your job is literally online, it's so easy to be connected to work and distraction *all.the.time.* I'm working, right? And, legit, Stevie and I are. But we have to disconnect from those devices sometimes.

Our travels make this more obvious to Stevie and me. When we leave the United States and go to Europe, people just don't seem to be on their phones as much. Especially when they're at the park with their family or out with their friends. It's almost like I don't realize how much I'm on my phone until I'm immersed in a culture that . . . isn't.

Here's the good news: You don't have to haul yourself across the Atlantic to put your phone down. But what about the other things we're connected to? This problem isn't new. Long before computer technology, humans struggled with distractions.

I'll tell you a big one for me. I can be super connected to saying yes.

Someone says, "Hey, do you want to go to this thing on such-and-such date?" and before I've even really thought about it . . . wham! I've sent a wire out to that thing, connecting myself.

Do I really even want to go? Do I truly have time, based on what I say is most important to me?

Professionally, I've said yes to opportunities and brand collaborations without thinking about how it might pull me away from Stevie or the girls.

And when I've done it—connected myself to an obligation before I've even checked in with myself—the commitment costs me in other areas. So that's one area where I'm challenging myself. *Hey, Sazan, why not give yourself a minute? Don't say yes right off the bat. Take a beat. Think about what your schedule really looks like, and decide if your choice prioritizes your family and friends.*

I'm learning to disconnect myself from that reflexive yes. And guess what? There are people out there who still like me. I'm still having fun in my life. As it turns out, jumping the gun and saying yes to everything without thinking it through *isn't* the secret to happiness. Who knew?

Here's another one. A good connection. One I'm making on purpose.

On Wednesdays, I head out to my weekly chiropractor appointment. 'Cause your girl? She's got some aches and pains to deal with. So I go see my chiropractor all by myself, and then I make a run through Starbucks. It's the only time I hit Starbies during the week. I don't mess with my phone. I just go get adjusted. And get caffeinated.

This awesome little moment takes me out of the grind and provides me with some peace and grace.

Can I get an amen?

That simple little Wednesday routine? It makes me feel more connected to my life.

That's the irony of this whole thing with disconnecting and connecting. All those things you're connected to? *They can disconnect you from your life! From your people.* Seriously! I bet you've been in the middle of an event, a conversation, or an experience, but you're so in your own head or on your phone that you might as well have stayed home.

We gotta show up for our lives.

.   .   .

There's magic in meandering.

Now, listen, I love to plan and schedule. Planning is important. I do think that getting an agenda on paper is a good way to be intentional about getting the good stuff done.

But . . .

I can get too connected to that schedule. The hurry. The moving from one thing to the next without even stopping for a breath.

Since when did I make it a crime to take five minutes between projects?

So in the midst of being intentional with my time and not letting it just slip through my fingers, I'm also figuring out how to let go. A little. I need to stretch the muscle that pulls the wire that keeps me tethered to the calendar and clock.

And unplug that wire every now and then.

Sometimes unplugging looks like heading out to the playset with the girls, sitting in their little fort, and letting them bring me teacups made of acorns. Sometimes it looks like heading up to the playroom and painting with them. Sometimes it looks like wandering through a new part of town.

It's disconnecting from the familiar or the expected. And connecting to something a little different.

Disconnecting is not a passive movement. I'm moving from one action to another. I'm disconnecting from one thing so I can connect somewhere else. That's probably the part where I got confused for a while. I'd say I needed to disconnect, so I'd put down the phone, bail on the invite, whatever.

Then I'd veg out.

I am a world champion vegger when I want to be. And doing nothing can be good for us.

But disconnecting is about making room for something else to connect to. Do you know what I mean? If the only time I disconnect is to simply disconnect from everything, then I'm missing a golden chance to connect with my people. With my life. With what matters.

I love that for nine months each, my girls were connected to me through their umbilical cords. How amazing. We were all wired up together. My body was meeting their needs through their placentas and umbilical cords, and they were connected to me to meet those needs.

But once they were born? They were disconnected physically from me. I mean, of course, I'm still obsessively connected to my girls (especially Amari's cheeks and Teeny's need for stick-on face jewelry). But the umbilical cords had served their purpose. They had served the need. It was time to disconnect from the girls in that way so I could connect with them as they grow and change.

Look, there are probably some things out there that you're still connected to that have been good for you. But maybe, just maybe, is it time to see if that cord, that thing that binds you, is serving you? Do you need it? Or is it just a habit? Or a guilt trip?

What is serving you well right now? And what needs to go? Is it that group you've been hanging out with? Is it an attitude that holds you back instead of connecting you to your future? There's good in letting go.

·   ·   ·

I don't care what the research says.

I am a multitasker. And I know, there are all these researchers out there saying that multitasking is not a thing. And I say, "Hello? Have you met this group of people called *moms*? 'Cause those people multitask. The end."

But . . .

I'm taking my disconnecting up a notch these days. On occasion, I'm disconnecting from my multitasking ways. And I'm connecting to one thing. At a time. *Just one thing.*

What is this madness? I know.

One example is when I'm making dinner. I love to cook. I love to dream up meals. I love to feed my family. And I know that if I don't disconnect from all the stuff and connect to what I'm doing, things can go sideways fast. Salt gets confused with sugar. Pot roasts burn. Fingertips get chopped. *Ahem.*

You know what I mean.

So I connect to one thing at a time. You gotta pay attention in the kitchen. Making the broth. Dicing the carrots. Chatting with Stevie. Rinsing the mixing bowl. Each step resets the rhythm of the evening. It connects me back to the family after a workday of juggling nine things at once.

It connects me to the goodness of this moment.

Do it for yourself. Take on something that forces you to focus on one thing at a time. Follow the recipe. Take the pottery class. Read the book. And do *only* that.

Look, things will inevitably pull on your attention—things you don't even mean to spend time on. You need to know it. I need to know it. We have to look for the things that are trying to drag us away from seeing and experiencing our lives.

Stevie told me about this awesome conversation he got to have with John Eldredge, a spiritual teacher we both respect and admire. He told Stevie that a lot of people know something's not right in their lives, but they don't know what's wrong. They don't know how to fix what's going on in their hearts.

But one of the graces God gives is beauty, and observing beauty on a daily basis helps heal our souls. When we take in beauty, the experience attaches us to something better, something bigger.

Guess what? Beauty isn't in your cell phone. You won't find it in your hectic schedule. And it sure as heck isn't in that true-crime series you're bingeing.

Beauty is in Teeny's closet playland. It's in a baby curled up on your chest. It's in slow moments you savor. It's in taking five minutes to go look at the sky. That's how we heal our souls. It's how we heal our relationships.

It's how we get untangled. It's how we reconnect with our Creator. What you're looking for, what I'm looking for, isn't found in the distractions. It's in the things that just quietly *are* and don't fight for our attention.

> **When we take in beauty, the experience attaches us to something better, something bigger.**

That means I've got to fight for them. I'm going to do battle to hold onto the beauty. To not get lost in the busyness. To connect to my Creator, to my community, and to what I value.

Next time you find yourself doing three tasks at a time, jumping from one thing to the next without a break, or next time you feel overwhelmed, take a breath and disconnect. All it takes is a minute's walk outside. Play peekaboo with a baby or listen to a beautiful piece of music. And what comes back down the wire to you is what you've been looking for: a joyful peace that is yours to have.

CHAPTER 11

SHOW UP AND GATHER

It was 2008, the evening before Christmas Eve.

In Christmas math, that means it was December 23.

I (Sazan) had just turned nineteen a few weeks before, and I was living in Dallas, Texas, with my family. I was a teller at a bank. Yes, your girl Sazan was working at a bank. And while I tried to be the friendliest teller you ever did meet, I can't say a career in banking and finance seemed to be the best fit for me. Turns out, banking is more about working with numbers than working with people and stories and my general Sazaniness. Though I may have been Dallas's friendliest teller, banks tend to be pretty particular about numbers.

It's a lot, I know.

But life was good. I was figuring out college classes and work. And it was my very favorite time of year: Christmas. Our family always celebrated with tons of gatherings and food and presents.

As is pretty typical in Dallas around the holiday season, the weather had actually been fairly warm and nice. My youngest brother, Rejiar, whom we call JiJi, had been playing that afternoon in the December sunshine in shorts, running off some energy before the evening's plans. JiJi is almost twelve years younger than me, so he was eight years old at this time.

It was my sister Stran, two years older than me, who noticed first. "Mom," she asked our mother as she and JiJi came into the house, "what are those bruises JiJi has? They're all over him!"

My mom gave him a quick look. "He's always running and playing and falling. He's an eight-year-old kid. He's supposed to have some bumps and bruises."

At that point, my oldest sister, Sayran, entered the chat. During her high school years, she attended a magnet school with a focus on medical technologies. While she ultimately didn't pursue a career in medicine, she took her studies seriously and had a good understanding of symptoms worth paying attention to. She started looking at the bruises on JiJi's arms and legs.

She looked concerned as she pulled my mom, Stran, and me aside. "Those bruises are pretty nasty looking. They don't look like normal bruises. I really think you should get him to the doctor, Mom. He could have anemia or something."

Mom once again assured us. "He's just a busy, active kid. It's normal."

For whatever reason, my sisters and I just couldn't let it go, so we ganged up on her. "What would it hurt to just take him in for a quick checkup? Let them do a little blood work. If he's anemic, he needs some iron or something." We kept on and on.

Finally, I guess we wore her down. "Fine," she huffed. "I'll run him over to urgent care. There won't be any doctors' offices open this time in the evening." She hustled him into the car, ready to get us off her back, while the rest of us stayed back at the house, continuing to prep for Christmas.

At the urgent care clinic, the staff gave my brother the once-over. They took a look at his bruises, and they also noticed a few dots on his face that looked like possible burst capillaries—but those could have also just been signs of an eight-year-old boy yelling and playing and rough-housing. They decided to do a blood draw so they could identify any iron deficiencies or other issues. In and out, easy-peasy. Within a couple of hours, my mom and my brother were back at the house. We jumped back into Christmas activities.

And then the phone rang around eight o'clock. My mom answered.

It was the urgent care clinic.

"We got your son's blood results back," the nurse told her. "His red blood cell count is off, and his white blood cell count is really high, so it's clear his body is fighting some kind of infection. Or something else may be going on. We're going to refer you guys on to somebody who specializes in situations like this."

That referral ended up being to a pediatric oncologist.

Pure panic set in.

Not only were we getting this news cold, but we also found out we'd need to head to the pediatric oncologist's office at Medical City Dallas the next day.

On Christmas Eve.

Though my mom was terrified, she also kicked into gear. It was wild. On the one hand, she wanted us to knock out the next tests quickly. But her mindset was sort of like, *Let's get this done so we can move on with Christmas. We've got plans!* It seemed to be her way of both taking the next scary step while also still being in denial. Through it all, she was protective, loving, and devoted to JiJi.

The next day, my sisters, my dad, my mom, JiJi, and I all went to the doctor's office together, while my other brother, Sherwan, stayed back at the house with my aunt. It was a pretty quick visit because the doctor had received my brother's test results from the urgent care clinic. "Based on what I'm seeing, we need to run a bone marrow tap to get some more information on what's going on."

Sayran motioned Stran and me over to a quiet spot in the hallway. "Listen," she whispered. "We watched some bone marrow procedures back when I was in those medical courses. The process was really painful for the patients, so I'm worried about what JiJi might go through. And you need to know they do those bone marrow tests to see what kind of cancer someone might have. We need to be ready." Her warning jolted all three of us sisters into mama bear mode.

Thankfully, because he was a pediatric patient, JiJi would be put under light sedation for the procedure. I was glad he wasn't going to feel pain from the test, but I wasn't prepared for the moment they came into the room and gave him the sedation medication. In a matter of minutes, he went from an active little boy bouncing around on the hospital bed to slumped over in a medicated sleep.

Once they took him in for the bone marrow test, I had to do something with myself. Anything. I couldn't stand sitting in the uncomfortable waiting room chairs a minute longer. I grabbed my sisters, and we headed for a gift shop in the lobby. We wandered through the aisles, wondering, *What's the right stuffed animal to get a kid who could be looking at a horrible diagnosis? What balloons should we get?* We didn't want to buy anything that said "Get Well Soon" because we didn't want him to be sick and didn't yet know if he was. We quickly got overwhelmed and dissolved into tears.

The lady working the cash register came to see if we were all right. The three of us started talking over each other, explaining about JiJi and how he was currently undergoing a bone marrow tap. She listened, patted our shoulders, and handed us tissues. "It's going to be okay," she said. "No matter what, it's going to be okay." Those simple words, which didn't hold answers to our questions, helped hold us together. She seemed like a guardian angel to us, giving us compassion in the midst of our confusion and tears.

That afternoon, we waited at the doctor's office to learn what the bone marrow tap would reveal. The doctor entered the exam room, brisk and businesslike.

"We're looking at leukemia," he began. "It's in the bone marrow. We still have to determine what type it is, so we'll need to run a few more tests for that. We'll also need to do a spinal tap tomorrow morning to see if it's spread. We're moving you up to the sixth floor of the hospital."

The sixth floor was the children's oncology wing. We would not be putting things off for a few days so we could get through Christmas first. We were sent directly upstairs. My brother was now a cancer patient.

I know the doctor's approach might sound a little cold, but ultimately, I appreciated how he quickly got to the point. He said, "There are two things we need to find out. First, if he has ALL (acute lymphocytic leukemia) or AML (acute myeloid leukemia). We also need to see if it has spread beyond the bone marrow and determine how long it's been in your brother's system."

ALL is a highly treatable type of childhood leukemia with a 90 percent cure rate. If it was determined that my brother had ALL, he could be treated while living at home. If he had AML—well, that type of cancer is trickier. More deadly. And kids have to stay in the hospital for the duration of their treatment.

In the world of childhood leukemia, ALL is definitely the preferable type.

That became my prayer—that my brother's cancer would be ALL, not AML.

Around four p.m. that afternoon of Christmas Eve, the doctor showed back up to my brother's hospital room. Once again, he got right to it. "I know today has been a very emotionally packed day, and I know a lot's been going on with nurses coming in and out. I know we were all hoping that his type of cancer would be ALL, but it's not. It's AML." He told us my brother would need to undergo a spinal tap the next morning.

Christmas morning.

And because of the treatment protocols for AML cancers, that's when we realized: This hospital was going to become our home.

It would be our home for Christmas, and for however long my brother would need to stay here. No stockings. No dolma, the Middle Eastern dish my family loves to prepare for big family meals together. No extended family and friends dropping by the house for a special Christmas dessert. No afternoon naps. No game night after all the presents were opened.

I know it's often said that kids are resilient—that they don't yet understand the severity of tough situations. JiJi certainly was a resilient kid, but he understood far more of the impact of this diagnosis than most kids his age might've. Just a few years previous, we had lost my uncle to cancer. JiJi knew how sick my uncle had been, knew how brutal the treatments that my uncle underwent were.

JiJi began to cry. "I don't want to lose my hair," he sobbed. It was the first time we saw him break amid the chaos of the previous day. My whole family started crying with him. It was just too much seeing the beloved baby of the family, the one we were all crazy about, so terrified and hurting.

Sometimes, in the toughest of circumstances, you're given an extra measure of strength to share with someone else. You're given a grace to show up for them in the way they need. As scared as I was, and though I felt on the verge of shattering, JiJi's fear and tears ignited yet another level of strength in me. Though my heart was breaking, I also felt calm—and my sense of protectiveness reached a new tier.

"It's just hair," I told him. "It will grow back better than ever. You'll see."

That night, our whole family piled into the hospital room with JiJi. The movie *Stand by Me* played on the small television. We sat in that room together, staring at the screen, all of us in a state of shock. And when it was time for JiJi to get some sleep, my dad, sisters, and I made the drive back to our house, leaving our mom and JiJi at the hospital.

It felt like the longest drive ever.

When we arrived home, my dad care-fully placed his car keys on the small table in our entry. Then he sank into his chair at the table in our dining room. This room was normally filled with laughter and loud conversation and delicious food, particularly on the holidays. This evening, it was silent and foreboding.

> **Sometimes, in the toughest of circumstances, you're given an extra measure of strength to share with someone else.**

Would we ever have a family meal, a Christmas Eve dinner, with my baby brother again?

My dad lowered his face into his hands. And began to weep.

My sisters and I surrounded him, holding him in our arms. We clung to each other, crying, each of us praying in our own way. Our lives had been completely turned upside down in the last twenty-four hours.

And we knew so much more lay ahead of us.

I didn't have much of a personal relationship with God at that time. But I'm telling you, when something like this happens, when we go through our darkest times, our natural default as humans is to turn to our Creator. Whether we understand who God is or not, there's something so deep in us that seeks him for comfort and answers. I didn't really understand prayer. I was just hoping to get on some kind of waiting list—that maybe, just maybe, God might hear me out. *My brother's got cancer,* I prayed. *And this could end badly. I'm just asking that you, God, whoever you are, would give us good news tomorrow. Just please give us some good news. We need it.*

Christmas morning dawned.

Back to the hospital we went.

They wheeled JiJi back, and we waited. JiJi endured a spinal tap when he was supposed to be opening Christmas presents. I brought in the presents that were stacked outside of JiJi's hospital room, like each of the other children's rooms, as if Santa Claus had visited during the night. Other children had been in residence here for weeks, for months, as they underwent various cancer treatments. Worse, other rooms in the same hospital were being turned over because some children would never have another Christmas.

We watched the clock. We watched each other. JiJi came back from the spinal tap, and we stayed huddled there in his room, waiting to see what this day would hold.

Finally, one of JiJi's doctors came to the door.

"I have great news."

He had me at *great news.*

The cancer had not spread beyond the bone marrow. Eighty percent of his marrow was covered in blasts, which is what they call the cancer cells. That meant he would need chemo immediately and radiation in the near future.

But the cancer had spread no farther.

It was enough good news for us—a Christmas miracle bigger than anything I'd ever experienced. I'd never seen so much Christmas joy. We all cried and laughed and squealed with joy. Can I get an amen and a hallelujah for anybody who knows what it's like to see a little light peeking through when you're going through your darkest hour?

Forty-eight hours before, childhood cancer was the last thing on our minds. Now, on Christmas morning, we were cheering that the AML cancer attacking my brother's body was contained.

The doctors originally told us it would take up to six rounds of chemo to hopefully put JiJi in remission. But his recovery was nothing short of incredible. After just one round, which took thirty days, the chemo did its work. He was in remission. He went through two more rounds of chemo and also radiation just to make sure. Winter turned to the early days of spring as JiJi remained in the hospital, going through all the protocols.

JiJi's doctors told us the best-case scenario would be if he could receive a bone marrow transplant from a family member who was a match. His bone marrow had taken a major hit during the rounds of chemo; unfortunately, the treatments themselves can kill the bone marrow as well as the cancer cells. Because of this, a lot of cancer patients need bone marrow donation. A great marrow match for JiJi would help ensure his continued remission. And it could significantly reduce his chances of having this type of cancer ever again.

My sisters and I immediately signed up for bone marrow match testing. All three of us were shown to be possible matches, which meant we moved on to the next round of testing.

Bone marrow is an incredible substance. It's the spongy material in your spine. It's in your elbows and your skull. It's in the core of your bones. It's the factory of your blood cells: your red blood cells, which carry oxygen throughout your body; the platelets that help your blood clot when you're bleeding; and the white blood cells, which help you fight infections. As such, it's the foundation of your immune system. Bone marrow is even mentioned in the Bible: "For the word of God is alive and active. Sharper than any double-edged sword, it penetrates even to dividing soul and spirit, joints and marrow; it judges the thoughts and attitudes of the heart" (Hebrews 4:12).

Bone marrow matching works on a system of points. The more points you have matching the person who needs the transplant, the better the outcome. My sister Stran ended up being a four-out-of-six match.

Now it was up to Sayran and me. I remember telling Sayran to switch spots with me in the testing lineup; for some reason, I felt a strong pull to go to bat next.

I was a six. Which meant I was the best "perfect six-six" match for my brother.

I was beyond elated. Finally, I had a way to show up for him that would literally be bone-deep.

I was put to sleep for the bone marrow extraction, and my marrow was placed in an IV bag. Then my brother was prepped to receive my marrow. My mom prayed over that bag, and the drip began. There's always a chance that a patient's body will reject the marrow, and people spend months waiting anxiously and hoping the transplant takes. So many patients get to the point of remission (including my very own uncle) and go through the transplant process with compromised immune systems that need to build back up. Many families and donors have witnessed their bone marrow not being "good enough" or efficient enough to fight off high-risk infections. Miraculously, my brother's system accepted my donation.

Prior to the bone marrow transplant, his blood type was B-positive. Now it's B-negative, just like mine. His dark hair grew back in, but it came in curly, just like mine. And, hello, who wouldn't want this texture? We were now bone marrow twins, or, as we like to call ourselves today, BMTs.

That hospital room, the one we'd first moved into on Christmas Eve, became a sanctuary of sorts for my family. I would have never thought it would come to feel like home, but it did for more than three months. It felt like a home because my family all showed up for each other there. There were days each of us felt strong and felt we could be strong for JiJi. On other days, we helped prop each other up when the stress became too much. We put our lives on hold to show up for each other. I put a pause on school, and as soon as I got off work at the bank, I'd go straight to the hospital.

My brother's cancer journey impacted all of us. For me, I learned just how fragile and precious life truly is. Because of the experience, I ultimately got honest with myself that a career in banking was not my purpose. It gave me the courage to pursue my dreams, to build my own thing.

Even more, that whole experience—having our typical life come to a screaming halt, then transitioning our home life to a hospital—showed me what it looks like to be there for others when things get rough. Some people show up during hard times, and some people won't. I want to be the kind of person who shows up for my people.

Pay attention to who shows up for you. The people who stick by you when the going gets tough. In turn, show up for your people. There are times it will be scarier than you ever could have imagined. And yes, it will hurt at times.

But I can tell you that the good life can be found in a hospital room on the darkest Christmas Eve. It can be found in the moments when you cling to each other, when you have no idea what the next day will hold.

Showing up for each other is underrated. In the small moments, like celebrating a good grade on a report card. In the big moments, like huddling together in a pediatric oncology hospital room. There's something about showing up, even when you feel like you can't make much of a difference.

I have this idea that showing up for each other is like being willing to see if you're a bone marrow match. Sometimes, proof that you've been willing to put in the time speaks volumes to someone.

And sometimes, you're just the thing someone needs to breathe life back into their bones.

Through my brother's cancer journey, we learned about the bone

> **There's something about showing up, even when you feel like you can't make much of a difference, that does.**

137

marrow matching opportunities available.* Unfortunately, cancer patients are always waiting for their match and looking to registries if they don't have a family member option. I feel it in my heart to share that anyone and everyone can undergo a simple test and have their information held in a database for a cancer patient who might be a match. It's a simple swab kit you can send off in the mail. It's how I want to live—ready to show up for my community's little events and big ones, ready to be a match in someone's life. It's how I hope my community will show up for me.

. . .

JiJi is now twenty-two years old. He's pursuing his dreams of film and television out in Los Angeles, yet another thing that makes us feel like bone marrow twins. It's incredible how his cancer journey inspired me to chase my dreams in media, and now he's chasing his own in the same industry. He's healthy. He's a ton of fun. He's still my baby brother, but he's a man now. I know his story isn't how it turns out for everyone, and my heart aches for you if you've experienced a different outcome.

But here's what I know now. Being part of a family, having friends like family, is about being there for each other. Being together is one of the most healing and impactful things we can do, however the story turns out.

If you don't know what to do when hard things happen in your group, show up.

If you don't know what to say, show up.

If you don't think you can make a difference, show up.

When we show up for each other, even when we don't have the answers, even when a situation is beyond our understanding, good things happen.

Show up. One day at a time.

---

* I have been so fortunate to work alongside Be The Match to bring awareness to bone marrow matching. To find out more about the Be The Match organization, visit BeTheMatch.org, or you can register to become a bone marrow donor through my link: https://join.bethematch.org/sazan.

CHAPTER 12

GRIEVE, CELEBRATE, AND GATHER

The sun was setting in a blaze of orange and pink in the western sky. At least the sliver of it I (Sazan) could see from my tiny central Los Angeles apartment. I'd moved in a few months before, ready to toss my dreams into the Hollywood game of horseshoes. I was hoping to score some opportunities that would make this move worth it.

About twenty minutes to the north, Stevie was living his best life up in Woodland Hills. We had both moved out to California in

January 2013, each of us trying to make good on what we'd said we wanted to chase during our media/television degree program at UNT.

Stevie's birthday was fast approaching, right after the beginning of the new year in 2014. I wondered what this year might hold for us. For our ambitions and careers. For our futures.

What I did know was that in the past year of all things unfamiliar, Stevie had been my familiar place, something from home. Yet the relationship seemed stagnant, like it wasn't going anywhere. Sometimes we seemed to be treading water. At other times, I felt I had no right to try to push for a deeper romance since I knew I couldn't tell my family about him. Neither of us had put a stake in the ground or dropped a pin where this relationship would land. But through it all, one truth was always front and center.

I knew Stevie had my back. I knew, no matter what, that I had someone a twenty-minute drive away who was in my corner, someone who would come help me for any reason, at any time. And in that season of so many unknowns, I was incredibly thankful for that. We were going through many of the same struggles as we chased our dreams. We understood what the other was going through. While I wasn't sure what our love story might or might not hold, I knew I had an exceptional friend in Stevie. He was my *best* friend.

That's why I wanted to do something special, something thoughtful for his birthday.

But it couldn't be expensive.

Really, if possible, I needed it to cost nothing at all. Because starving artist vibes and all that. Enter Pinterest. I started looking for "thoughtful, unique, cheap gift ideas" and came up aces.

I found a post about creating thoughtful envelopes with customized messages inside. On the envelope, you'd write things like, "Open when you're feeling sad one day," or "Open when you're celebrating a big win."

Things like that. Inside each envelope, you'd include a card with a special message of encouragement or best wishes, depending on the event for each envelope.

The idea met my criteria perfectly. It was thoughtful, meaningful, and fit my budget of exactly zero dollars. Talk about a win-win.

I also knew this idea would really work with Stevie's personality. He has such an honest heart that I knew he would wait to open each envelope until his day matched the instructions written on the front of each one.

Sidenote: I don't think this would have worked the other way around, had Stevie given me a stack of such envelopes. Because, honey, I do not like surprises. And I am a person who, if given a bundle of envelopes like that, would definitely open them all in a single night.

I dug through some drawers and found a pack of rainbow-colored envelopes. Then, in a bag of school supplies from my university days, I found a package of index cards from when I used to make flash cards for studying. I grabbed the first marker I could find that wasn't all dried-up: a pink highlighter. Like, *neon* pink. Whatever. It would work.

I made several of the envelopes pretty quickly, coming up with occasions like, "Open when it's raining" and "Open when you're missing Texas." But after a while, I got stuck, and I still had a couple of envelopes to go. Back to the internet I went for inspiration. I scrolled through a few options.

Then this one popped up.

And hit me right in the heart.

"Open on your wedding day."

The words stopped me right in my tracks. Suddenly there was a lump in my throat. My heart started pounding. I couldn't really identify exactly what I was feeling, but it felt a lot like anxiousness. Like there was a lot on the line.

It felt . . . scary. My pulse would throb, and I would feel excitement. And then in the next throb, terrified. It was a wild, emotional ride.

On the one hand, I thought I should do it—write something on a card for Stevie's wedding day. After all, there was a slim chance it might be my wedding day too. On the other hand, things were just so complicated and so uncertain. It wasn't up to me to decide whom Stevie would ultimately marry.

There's no way, I thought to myself. *There's no way that I should even waste an envelope.* If I wasn't in the picture, he wouldn't even get around to opening this one. I mean, it would be pretty weird for him to save it for his wedding to another girl.

Oh, this? Yeah, it was a gift from one of my former girlfriends. I was supposed to save it for today.

Boy gets ditched at the altar.

And what would I even write on the card? Did I have a right to say anything to Stevie about his future wedding if I wasn't the one marrying him?

Yet that little sunshine yellow envelope and blue-striped index card seemed like an invitation. An invitation to hope. An invitation to write something down, in that pink highlighter, that would be a mini declaration to myself. A declaration of how I truly felt about him. A statement about what the future could look like.

I was already in LA, putting all my chips on the table. I had come so far to chase my professional dreams. Why not go ahead and, in this secret moment, go all in for what I hoped for in my personal life?

So I did it. I wrote "Open on your wedding day" on the envelope. And I wrote a short message on the index card in highlighter pink. I slid the index card into the envelope. Then I sealed the envelope, heart pounding, and put it at the bottom of the stack. It felt like an oath, like a challenge—a message in a bottle sent out into the waves of possibility.

"We'll see what happens," I told that little yellow envelope. "Maybe I'll see you again someday."

I bundled up the whole collection of envelopes and tied the stack together with twine. It was pretty homespun looking, but it was heartfelt.

I still remember the look on Stevie's face when I handed the bundle to him a few days later at his birthday dinner. "You bring so much color to my life," I explained to him, pressing the packet of rainbow envelopes into his hands. "I wanted to do something special for you. You're going to have all these experiences on different days in your life, and I want you to be able to turn to these envelopes right when you need them most."

Stevie read the top envelope, with its instructions about when to open it. He was so excited. It wasn't just a gift for this one day; it was a gift for all kinds of "one days." Days of happiness, days of challenge. The present would be present when he needed it. He was so appreciative, really taking in the intentionality of the gift.

Now, while your boy Stevie is absolutely thankful for thoughtful things, he's also known for losing things. A lot. Such as his keys (practically on the daily). So I made my peace with the fact that he might set the envelopes aside and then forget where he'd put them. But for several weeks after receiving the notes, he really did use them. True to his loyal nature, he only opened an envelope when it matched the kind of day he was having.

He really utilized what I had written. He would take a picture and send it to me when he opened one of the envelopes, which was so cool of him. The gift became something really sweet in our relationship. That little recycled Pinterest idea really worked.

· · ·

A year and a half after that birthday of Stevie's, life for both of us had radically changed. I'd conquered my greatest fear—the thing that had held me back from fully committing to a relationship with Stevie. I'd finally told my parents about him. And they had disowned me. Stevie and I were now on the fast track to the altar, and we were planning a wedding in just a handful of weeks. Looking back, I think it was God's way of keeping my mind distracted and off the aftershocks that ripped through my family following my announcement. I was knee-deep in wedding details, and I was also working a ton since Stevie and I would be on the hook financially for our wedding.

Now, we were only a few days away from being married.

That last week before the wedding, I began moving my stuff into Stevie's apartment. Stevie and I never lived together before getting married, so we had a lot to go through, to figure out what to keep. Did we actually need two cheese graters? And why, exactly, would Stevie need four baseball gloves? Clearly, some stuff needed to go. The Sazan Shoe Collection was going to need *space*. And while Stevie surely didn't need multiple baseball gloves, I absolutely *needed* four different styles of nude pumps, *thank you very much*. I was there by myself that day, and needless to say, I was feeling pretty overwhelmed by the stacks I still needed to go through.

So many boxes. So much unpacking. Our two worlds were coming together, and it was taking me forever to sift through all of my stuff and his, making room for the life we were going to build together.

I was working through a bunch of boxes in the second bedroom of the apartment when I opened a box full of picture frames. As I debated which ones to keep or donate, I noticed a shoe box at the bottom of the box. I reached for it and pried open the lid. Inside was a stash of Stevie's personal stuff. I didn't want to snoop or rummage around in his things. But then I saw it.

The corner of a sunshine yellow envelope.

It was peeking out from the bottom of the box underneath the stack of envelopes Stevie hadn't opened yet. There it was—a splash of yellow, a limelight of lemon.

It was as though God wanted me to see it, in that moment, on that day.

I pulled that yellow envelope from the stash. *Long time no see,* I thought.

It's wild how you can forget something—forget it for a long time. But when it reappears, the impact is huge. When that envelope reappeared that day, with its secret message hidden inside, I was taken right back to the moment I wrote it. To the moments when I didn't know if Stevie and I would ever work out. To the moments of laughter. To the moments we cried in frustration. To all the moments it took to get to *this* moment.

Every feeling, every frame of the film of our memories came back to me in a flash. I sat for a solid fifteen minutes with that yellow envelope in my hand. It was a holy moment, as gratitude and an incredible sense of the faithfulness of God filled my heart. Tears rolled down my cheeks while I whispered words of thankfulness.

I knew Stevie had to see this envelope. *Maybe I should call him. Maybe I should text him a picture.*

No.

Something even better.

I grabbed the envelope and walked into the room where Stevie's new tailored suit for the wedding was hanging in a garment bag, then slid the zipper on the side of the bag down a few inches. I reached into the garment bag, envelope in hand.

I slipped the envelope inside the pocket of Stevie's wedding day suit.

· · ·

There are times of grieving in the good life. There are times of celebrating in the good life. Sometimes those seasons run with clean borders,

> **There are times of grieving in the good life. There are times of celebrating in the good life. Sometimes those seasons run with clean borders. But sometimes, they run together.**

one following another, a tough season followed by a peaceful one. But sometimes, they run together.

Gathering together for an important life event or a holiday can really bring that swirl into full view. As Stevie and I prepared for our wedding, grief and celebration were often mixed. I was heartbroken that my parents wouldn't attend our wedding. I was thrilled to become Stevie's wife. I was so happy for all the love and support his family and our friends were giving us. I was sorrowful that I had been abandoned by several of my own relatives. The day of our wedding highlighted both the joy of gathering with those ready to bless our new marriage and the absence of others we loved who weren't ready to embrace our relationship.

What I discovered in that season is that the highest of highs and the lowest of lows sometimes happen at the same time. It doesn't make sense, and the extremes can yank your heart back and forth. You may struggle to know if the tears you're crying are happy, grateful tears or jagged tears of grief. I was marrying the man I'd dreamed of, but I wasn't having the wedding of my dreams because some of the people I loved most in the world were refusing to attend.

Sometimes, right in the thick of your very good life, you might just have to leave room in your heart to feel it all. Sometimes you have to gather those mixed emotions and hold them close, even when it feels like they shouldn't be held in the same space.

You know what really important lesson I learned in the middle of all this? I learned not to let the joy of my upcoming wedding keep me from the business of mourning the fractured relationship with my parents. I needed to be thankful for those who were standing with us as a community, gathering to lend their support. I also had to learn how to keep the happiness, the celebration of our love, vibrant and strong, despite the loss I was feeling. And I lived in hope that, one day, this promise of God might come to pass: "I will gather still others to them besides those already gathered" (Isaiah 56:8).

In that season, I could have fallen for the lie that everything was *ruined, ruined, ruined* because it wasn't all *perfect, perfect, perfect*.

Instead, God in his grace taught me to let those two streams—those tributaries of celebration and grief—overflow their banks and combine their forces. The clear, bright waters of celebration swirled into the current that carried the dark, murky depths of grief. They tumbled and danced, pushing downstream in a river of life.

Because that's what life is. A blend.

The Monica Geller in me would prefer to keep such contrasting emotions in separate containers. I'd like to think of the inside of my heart as a carefully organized drawer with nice rectangular bins lined up in a row, emotions sorted by category. Then I'd only dip into the utensil drawer of feelings for the specific dish life was serving me up at the moment. But sometimes my or other people's decisions or wild circumstances dump the drawer, and everything tumbles together. Soupspoon next to pie server.

Ecstatic next to sad. And you need them both for what's on the current menu.

Don't be afraid to experience both. I promise, doing so makes it all more powerful. More real. Gather it all up. It makes you strong. It is good. That's what I want you to know.

. . .

The day of our wedding. Finally.

I was getting ready as brides do. It was a full-day thing, from exfoliating to lashes.

Stevie, why don't you tell our lovely reader what you were up to?

STEVIE'S POV

Well, I'd been in Vegas for my bachelor party, and I came skidding back into Los Angeles just in time to run to my apartment and grab my clothes for the ceremony. I hurried inside and took the garment bag with my suit. I was—*ahem*—trying to beat (and by *beat* I mean *bludgeon*) the clock, rushing to our wedding venue. Our wedding was soon, set for the early evening.

Pro tip for the people in the back: Don't fly in from Vegas a couple of hours ahead of your wedding. You're welcome.

Once I got to the venue, I went to the groom's room to get dressed. I caught my breath after the hurry from the airport to the apartment and then from the apartment to the Airbnb. I changed into my dress pants and crisp new shirt. I got my tie on straight and slipped on my shoes. I gave the ol' hairdo a quick check in the mirror.

Then I put on my suit coat.

That's when I found it. A yellow envelope, peeking out of my suit coat pocket.

I pulled out the envelope and read the words printed on it. I recognized it immediately as one of the envelopes from Sazan from that birthday long ago. I sank down on the bed, clutching the envelope in my hands.

"Open on your wedding day."

I flipped the envelope over and slid my finger under the seam on the back. I pulled the index card out.

And I started to weep. Big tears.

It had been such a long road. At times, it had seemed impossible.

My mom came in to check on me, making sure I was on schedule. She found me, all right—right in the middle of a puddle of tears. "What is it?" she soothed. "What's going on? You know you're going to have a beautiful life together."

I handed her the envelope and the index card, the one Sazan had written one day long ago. The one she had written when everything was so confusing. The one she had written before she went against her culture and her parents' wishes.

The one I realized she must have written in a moment of profound honesty with herself, even when our future seemed bleak.

My mom and I looked down together at the card, at the five words written in pink highlighter. Words that acknowledged potential heartbreak. Words that longed for joy.

"I hope it was me."

NIGHTTIME
REST

Rest feels like something that should happen when everything is shut down for the night. The windows are latched, Sweetie the golden retriever has gone out for one more bedtime piddle, and the lights are low.

"'Twas the Night before Christmas" kind of stuff. Not a creature was stirring, not even a teeny (Teeny) restless preschooler.

Cozy, quiet, safe. Tucked in.

And that certainly is one of my favorite forms of rest.

But God's been teaching me (Stevie) through the years that rest can look a lot of different ways while still being rest. Rest can be coming to a full stop for a day to catch your breath. Rest can be taking a break from screens. Rest can be taking a few minutes in a busy day to say a prayer, pause, and move on.

Here's what I'm learning. Rest's primary ingredient is . . . trust.

Sazan and I both love to work out. We like the discipline. We like that it gives us the energy to keep up with our girls. And every so often, I'll decide I've got a new fitness goal, such as lifting a heavier amount of weight or adding some time to my cardio. We've got great friends and trainers who share helpful information about taking our routines to the next level. And one thing they always say—the advice that never seems to make sense no matter how many times I hear it—is the importance of rest days.

"Those are the days you're gaining muscle," they'll say. "During rest, your body is rebuilding."

Yeah, that doesn't really sound like a thing. Just trust that my body is doing what it's supposed to, even though I'm not out there busting it every single workout session? That can't be right.

But it is.

I have to trust that rest also does its work.

When people ask me about my faith, I can't wait to share with them that God is there when we take big steps of faith. During the times when it feels like we're out on the wire without a net, he does some incredible things. Even then, God says we can rest. And I have to trust that the God who created rest has a reason for it and that reason is for my good. And for your good too.

When the stress is building and the stakes are high, rest can feel like the last thing you should be doing. But as each day turns from day to night, even the act of getting ready for bed, checking the doors, and turning down the lights can be a moment to remember.

Rest is there, ready to receive you. Rest is ready to welcome you home.

CHAPTER 13

REST IN BEING ENOUGH

O ne day," I (Stevie) would say. "One day, I'm going to Norway."
And I wasn't even trying to rhyme.

Why Norway? I'm glad you asked. Do I have ancestral roots there? Not that I know of. Do I have lifelong friends who moved there and who have been telling me I need more fjords in my life? Nope. Do I think Norway is the next place to invest in some entrepreneurial opportunity? Not a clue.

No, my Norway dreams had to do with a particular conversation I had with my dad one night.

Every Thanksgiving night, after all the food, after the cleanup, and after the rest of the family goes into their post-turkey comas, my dad and I have a little tradition. We escape to the back porch, unwrap our Thanksgiving cigars, light 'em up, and talk. It's a thing. We have a great talk about life, catching up on all the things that are currently going on in our lives, our marriages, and what God is teaching us.

During this particular Thanksgiving cigar hang, my dad suddenly jumped topics and said, "Man, Norway is one place I still need to take you boys. I went once after I graduated college, and it was incredible."

And just like that, my need to go to Norway appeared on the dashboard and kept blinking like a "change oil" light in my mom's minivan. Norway. I needed to go.

I was raised by a couple of adventurers. My dad, whom we call Pop, was raised as an Army brat. He spent his childhood moving back and forth between Maryland and Germany. I grew up hearing stories of his time living in Germany, where on Boy Scout trips, he would ski in the Alps. My mom, growing up in Norfolk, Virginia, came from a tough family situation of divorce. She wasn't as well-traveled, but I swear it made her all the more adventurous for it. I remember as a kid I would call our minivan the "raging minivan" because my mom was determined to push that minivan to the max, hence the constantly blinking "change oil" light. Both my parents have a strong love for adventure. And I got a double dose, having inherited it from both of them.

·   ·   ·

A few months went by after that conversation with my dad, months filled with a lot of change for Saz and me. I was now a new father, and while that was for sure a new adventure, the rhythms of life with a newborn meant I was locked into a more domestic cycle. Everything was sweet and great. But as the months went by, I started to feel that itch to go, to explore.

Sazan and I are blessed to have been able to travel internationally quite a bit. Our work had taken us to all kinds of cool places. But that wasn't what I needed this time. I needed a trip that would be mine, one where I could kick the agenda to the curb. I was ready for some time to just go be a dude, to get my hands dirty.

So when Sazan asked me what I wanted for my upcoming birthday, my answer was crystal clear. "Babe, I don't want any stuff or surprises or a party. I want Norway."

And I knew who I wanted to go with me. Pop.

It took some planning—making sure Sazan had the help she needed with Teeny, and getting ahead on work projects so I could clear the calendar for a few days. But we figured it out, and my dad and I soon found ourselves in Bergen, Norway, greeted by incredible mountains, fjords, and the quaintest little colored buildings. The adventures started right away. Pop wanted us to spend the first night in the old youth hostel he had stayed in nearly thirty-five years earlier. All I can say is I don't think they had updated those bunks since he'd left in the mid-1980s.

We walked around the town and enjoyed our first Norwegian sunset on the docks. The next day, we made our way up to Lofoten, which is north of the Arctic Circle. And let me tell you a remarkable fact about this remote area. It may go without saying that the landscape was the most striking I've ever seen. But the cell service? Chef's kiss. Not even kidding. Here I was, at the literal top of the world in one of the remotest places imaginable, and I had five bars of service everywhere. Look, when you're in the influencer business, finding full-tilt cell service is always a thing of beauty.

The mountains were soaring, the cell service was popping, and the locals perfectly understood my native Texas language. Win, win, and win. What I didn't yet know about Lofoten, about the Arctic Circle, was that the place was about to teach me one of the most important lessons of my life.

As the end of our trip drew near, we planned to have dinner at a restaurant called Maren Anna. The restaurant is in Sorvagen, a small fishing village near the tip of the Lofoten archipelago. Maren Anna sits right on the water. It's in an old fishing shed, called a *rorbu*, painted a crisp barnyard red.

That night, when we arrived at the restaurant, a snowstorm had just blown in, so we were two of only nine people dining there that night, plus the manager and the waiter. The food was incredible. Want to know how many ways you can prepare cod? Apparently, a gazillion, based on the Maren Anna menu. I still think about their mouthwatering cod dishes. The storm blustered outside, butter and garlic and fresh-from-the-water fish perfumed the air, and the quiet chatter of our fellow diners cushioned us. It was a meal for the ages.

When we finished, I walked up to the bar to pay the tab. I noticed a piano up against the wall in the middle of the dining room. Any time I see a piano, I am curious to feel the keys, to hear how it sounds. To me, a piano is like a living thing, as if each piano has a unique soul. I asked the bartender if I could touch the keys. "Sure," he said. "You can play if you like." I didn't have any intention of playing; I just wanted to hear the piano's tone. But as I laid my hand on a few keys and played a few notes, the piano responded with a gentle, muted voice. It made me want to pull out the bench and linger for a while. I sat down and softly began to stroke the keys.

Now, I have to tell you that I am not a good piano player. I cannot read music, and I only took lessons for a short time as a kid. Regardless, I love to play, and I have a handful of songs I've created over the years. I don't really play for anyone other than Sazan and the kids and a few members of my family. Doing so feels pretty vulnerable. But that night at the restaurant, I felt like nobody was really going to listen anyway. Some bright jazz played over the sound system, and the few people in the place seemed fully engaged in their conversations. I quietly began to play one of my songs, losing myself in the experience.

After a few minutes, I noticed the restaurant speakers had gone quiet. So had the diners. The room was now silent except for the song I was playing. And just like that, a wave of nervousness slammed into me.

This song was something so near and dear to my heart. I felt like I was baring my soul to a room of strangers. My fingers began to tremble, and I could *feel* all the mistakes I could make. I almost stopped playing.

I took a deep breath.

"No. I'm not going to be nervous. I'm going to play my song as best as I can," I whispered to myself. And there, in that remote rorbu, in the middle of a snowstorm, a personal miracle took place.

I felt a rush of confidence come over me as I played, and a delicate presence seemed to fill the room.

When I finished my song, I heard all ten people in the bar begin to cheer and clap for me. "We want more!" a table of new friends shouted at me.

I chuckled. "Really, that's all I've got, but thank you." As I said, it's not like I've got a whole collection at my fingertips. But I did have that one. I had that one to give.

As I looked around the room, everyone was smiling at me, including Pop.

After thanking the group, I made my way to the door with Pop. Waiting there for me was a man and his wife. The man's face was full of emotion, his eyes rimmed in red. He was fighting back tears. He looked me in the eye and shook my hand. "Thank you," he said simply.

It was the most genuine, heartfelt thank-you I think I've ever received.

As we drove back to our hotel, my dad said, "You know, when you were playing in there, it felt like God's presence filled the room."

"I could feel it!" I replied. "I wondered if anyone else could."

"They could," he assured me. "It was special."

On the drive that night from Maren Anna, I realized the importance of sharing your gifts with the world. As I said, I'm no accomplished pianist, but I do have a deep love for music. I played my song that night in that small restaurant, and it made a difference to the eleven people there, including me.*

It made an impact.

I was thousands of miles away from home. But I was home in this moment, with these people I'd just met, because God took this moment to draw us all over the threshold. And when I laid my head on the pillow that night at the hotel, I experienced the kind of rest that comes when your offering—meager as it might feel—is enough.

You might have a hidden talent no one knows about. You may question if God has given you any significant gifts. I've often wondered if the gifts that God gave me would ever make a difference. Far too frequently we let our talents lie dormant under a rug of insecurity because we are too scared to unmask the beautiful mess underneath. My song that night was raw, unpolished, and full of emotion. And it was true. It was me.

> Far too frequently we let our talents lie dormant under a rug of insecurity because we are too scared to unmask the beautiful mess underneath.

If I had to give that song a title, I think it would be called "Enough." I've struggled, and maybe you have, too, wondering if my efforts are enough. If my skills or talents are enough. If I'm enough.

It's one of the deeper lies that has often kept me from recognizing my good life, even when I'm in the middle of living it. I've put off saying something or offering something because I stand back, hand on my chin, analyzing. I look at what I'm

---

* We've recorded "Enough" since I played it in front of that restaurant audience. It's featured on the A Real Good Life playlist on Spotify. You can find it with the QR code on page 211.

about to say or do and study it like I'm some kind of art critic. *I've seen better*, I'll think. *This will get me laughed out of the room.*

But here's the deal: I'm the only one who's saying it's not enough. Why? Because I'm already anticipating defeat. I assume others might say it's not enough, so I'm beating them to the punch.

Thinking you, your writing, or your business idea isn't enough is a way to hide in plain sight. When I'm not willing to take the risk to put something out there, no matter how someone else might judge it, I've already made the call. And here's where it gets all meta and ironic: When I decide ahead of time that I'm not enough or what I have to offer isn't enough, so I don't offer it, I've then fulfilled that narrative—that *I'm not enough*. It's like setting up some kind of crazy algebra problem where, in trying to solve it, I keep reducing myself. *I'm not enough* plus *they'll think I'm not enough* times *I won't take the risk of them seeing I'm not enough* equals *now I feel even more like I'm not enough.*

More not enough. How's that for a weird, inverted formula?

Here's what I learned that night at Maren Anna. I was enough. It didn't matter that I'm not a concert pianist. It didn't matter that I can't read music to save my life and that I don't know legato from mezzo from—heck—LEGOs. None of that has to do with what is enough. The willingness to take something simple, something kind, something heartfelt, and to offer it—*that* is enough.

We've got big problems in this big world of ours. And I feel like I don't have big solutions or big resources or big wisdom to give. But giving somebody a break is enough. Sharing an encouraging thought with someone is enough. Hey, even being vulnerable enough to say to someone, "I struggle with feeling like I'm enough. I want you to know that you are enough"—well, that's some serious treasure right there.

Remember that song from *The Greatest Showman*, where Rebecca Ferguson, who plays Jenny Lind, steps onstage and sings "Never Enough"? Sure, the lyrics can be understood as a love song, but the song hits different for me. It sounds like the anthem of our lives—that no matter how much good there is, we're always searching for more. That no matter how far we've come or what kind of progress we've made, we always see the gap. It's a powerful song. And it's a virus, a contagion, that we must contain. Because when you don't live believing you're enough and that your effort is enough, you spread that belief to others. You're measuring them and finding them wanting. You're missing what is sufficient in yourself and others and calling it scant.

Here's a little something you might not know. As convincing as Rebecca Ferguson looks when she's performing that song in *The Greatest Showman*, she is not actually the one singing the song. It was sung by the vocal artist Loren Allred and dubbed in.

Who's been singing the song in your life that you're never enough? And when did you start mouthing the words and making it your own?

It's not lost on me that the song I played that one night at Maren Anna doesn't have words. It has no lyrics. But at the same time, there's a whole story of feelings to that piece. And maybe that's part of the magic. What if you and I just played our songs? No lines of expectation. No angry lyrics about measuring up. What if we just sat down at the metaphorical pianos of life and gave from our hearts what we have to give?

Isn't that enough to a world desperate for beauty and peace and compassion?

And what if we performed that song in the context of our homes? What if our partners, our kids, and our golden retrievers heard a soundtrack in the background, every time they were around us, that resonated over and over: "You are enough. Enough is enough."

If you're waiting for the day when you'll feel like you're enough, lean in. That day is today.

Whatever you have accomplished today, it's enough.

Rest in that.

CHAPTER 14

REST IN SETTING OUT YOUR SEED

American white boy meets Middle Eastern brown girl. They fight for their forbidden love. They go against the expectations of their cultures. They marry. They have kids. They build a life.

Yep, it's a page from my and Sazan's romance. But it's also a page that was written in another story, one that paved the way for Sazan and me almost a hundred years ago.

In 1927 a young American named Bill was serving in the Navy in Tientsin, China. He loved the travel that his time in the Navy gave him. He loved to box, he loved art, he worked hard, and he chased adventure to experience new things. One day, he headed toward the racetrack for a military parade. He had no idea he would encounter the biggest adventure of his life.

Here's where we take a little world history break.

The country called Armenia is just over the border from Turkey. Some say the first leader of Armenia was a great-grandson of Noah. Yeah, *that* Noah—the one with the ark and the animals and the flood. And who knows? It could've been. Armenia is near Mount Ararat, the peak where the ark came to rest after the flood. Armenia is sometimes thought of as a European country because it adopted Christianity as a state religion in the fourth century, but by location and culture and tradition, it's a Middle Eastern nation made up of people of Middle Eastern heritage. To the north of Armenia is the country of Georgia.

From Armenian culture and heritage and living in Georgia came a young woman named Anya. She'd spent most of her life never being able to put down roots. Her family was under threat of the genocide taking place against the Armenian people. They had moved from place to place, from country to country—a family without a place to call home.

Anya was also at the parade in Tientsin that day in 1927.

Bill saw her. And she saw him.

Throughout the course of the day, their eyes kept finding each other through the crowd. Bill would feel her shy gaze come to rest on him, and he'd look at her. She'd give a small smile and modestly look away, only to glance over at him again.

When the parade ended, as the crowd began to thin out, they moved toward one another to meet. Face-to-face, the cheers of the crowd receding, the press of people around them easing. But what would they say to each other?

As it turned out, not much. Bill only spoke English, and Anya only spoke Russian, the most common language of Armenians in the modern era. They were really only able to communicate through looks, expressions, and rough attempts at impromptu sign language.

But their hearts? Their hearts understood each other perfectly. They were smitten. And their meeting that day in 1927 grew into a courtship.

They began to learn each other's languages. They learned the intricacies of each other's cultures. They wrestled with the doubts of their families and the prejudices against their union.

By 1929 they were married.

Their marriage encountered a lot of challenge. Bill remained in the Navy for the next two decades, and there were times when they were apart more than they were together. Anya had a whole lot to learn when she came to the States with Bill after their marriage. They set down roots in San Pedro, California, as a mixed-culture couple in the 1930s. Anya felt the culture shock of a completely new country, even having to adjust to a new name when they Americanized her name to *Anna*. There was the adjustment to being at home while Bill crossed the oceans of the world. I have to imagine that at times, it would have been easier to give up on their story. But they didn't. They stayed and fought for their love. They were married for forty-five years until Anna's passing.

> What they created was a legacy. They planted the seed for a coming generation.

What they created was a legacy. They planted the seed for a coming generation.

· · ·

Saz is all about making lists. And journaling. And scribbling in her planner. And creating reminders on Post-it Notes. We've got notebooks upon notebooks in this house, and they're mostly hers. I prefer a nice, clean note on my iPhone Notes app, you know what I'm sayin'? And Saz does that, too, keeping a whole bunch of stuff squirreled away on that phone of hers. But she also likes to use all these pens. "Oh, Stevie, you've got to feel the way this one writes! And look at that color of ink!"—*gasp!*—"The way this one flows across the page!" (Confession: They all look like pens to me. Just pens.)

As Teeny and Amari are growing and changing, Saz and I feel like we're starting to really get this parenting thing down—some days. On other days, the wheels come off. We love building this business together and having the girls along with us for the ride. Our kids get to see, in a way a lot of kids don't, what Mom and Dad's work world looks like and how we navigate our careers. I know it will serve them well to have grown up with this kind of experience.

But no joke, working mostly from home and having the girls around means we're constantly trying to balance the creative cycle with being engaged parents. Sometimes when the girls interrupt us, an idea we've been working on just—*poof!*—disappears somewhere into the Canyon of Lost Epic Ideas, never to be heard from again. Of course, our family is our priority. But making money to feed that family also seems like a pretty important thing to do. And I don't know what it is about some days, but sometimes deadlines and work stress collide with a Teeny temper tantrum or an Amari meltdown.

Like Saz shared earlier in the book, that's why she started thinking through setting up the next day for a win with the girls on the night before. And she does that with other things we have going on as well. She pulls out one of those notebooks and one of those pens at nighttime and gets to writing. Planning. Dreaming. She lists what she wants to accomplish the next day for content creation. She jots down stories she wants to share on socials. She comes up with a flow for the next day with the girls. And I've got to say that nighttime prepping really does help us stay focused on the good for the coming day.

We have a little garden patch in our backyard. It's fun to show the girls how to take care of plants and to harvest some herbs and little tomatoes. We've got a long way to go on our gardening chops, but we have a good time. When we started the garden, we planned what we wanted to grow. We took a look at what grows best in the Austin sunshine and heat. We read up on growing seasons. We set out our seed.

Some roses and tomatoes are heirloom plants that we want to include in our garden. The flowers and fruit have been cultivated for special qualities that have emerged in their generational line of plants. For brighter colors and bigger flavors. For more good today because of the good that has come before.

That's how I think about Sazan and the notebooks and those nighttime planning sessions. It's like she's sowing the seed for the next day—for what she wants to see grow in the lives of our kids and in our business. Right now, it feels like a day-to-day thing. And it is. But the longer we build these days, stacking them one upon the other, the more we start to see something taking shape. The life we're building takes on a contour. There are things happening each day that our girls will take with them into their own futures. I can imagine a day when I, all Stevie Silver Fox, go to one of my kids' houses and see a little schedule posted on the fridge for my grandkids. Just like their mom is doing for them now. And it's way more than a little list of what they'll be doing that day. It's a statement about how much they are loved. How much of a treasure this time is. How much good there is to experience. And it will have started from us trying to manage this day, speaking into a coming day. Because we've sown the seed.

. . . .

As that American white boy and that Armenian girl were falling in love at a parade in China, I'm sure they didn't think about their love story as some kind of treasure for someone in the future to inherit. But it's my inheritance. Bill and Anna are my great-grandparents.

Their determination to overcome cultural differences and family challenges was seed for a future harvest. When I fell in love with Sazan, I wasn't hanging it out there on my own. I was surrounded by the echo of Bill and Anna's love.

One of the epic verses in the Bible to me is this one: "Therefore, since we are surrounded by such a great cloud of witnesses, let us throw off everything that hinders and the sin that so easily entangles. And let us run with perseverance the race marked out for us, fixing our eyes on Jesus, the pioneer and perfecter of faith" (Hebrews 12:1–2). That's how I think about the impact of Bill and Anna's story in my own life; they're among that cloud of witnesses, cheering Sazan and me on. The combined DNA of their love runs through my veins. That's right; your boy Stevie had some Middle Eastern in him before he even met Sazan.

When I think about the good life, it's all too easy for me to focus on *my* good life. And, hey, I want the good life for me, and I want it for you. But I'm widening my understanding. There's an opportunity here. When I live my good life, I can pay it forward. I can hand down lessons I've learned. I can ready the ground for where a life after mine will be planted. Have you ever thought about that? When you live your life looking for the good, when you declare it good, you're holding up the light for those who come after you. And that doesn't mean you need to have kids or grandkids coming after you. Maybe some young woman will want to know your story. Someone may find your imprint online or in a journal entry, and as a result find the courage they need for the day they live in.

> **When I live my good life, I can pay it forward.**

More than ever before, what we're speaking now, what we're living now, is being captured for a coming generation. We've made and stored more images, more blogs, more vlogs, more podcasts than any generation before us. We'll be leaving an incredible collection of what it has meant to live during this time. We might have answers for questions that haven't even been asked yet. We'll be a voice outside of time, giving an account of our time in history—of what drove us, what we grappled with, where we found victory. I want to leave behind something from this good life— something that will give someone else a good life as well.

I never got to meet Bill and Anna Hendrix. They were gone before I was born. I look back through the ages at them through sepia-toned photographs, searching for the clues of their life and their love. There's one picture of them early in their romance, perched together, sitting at the base of a streetlamp—Bill in his Navy uniform grinning at Anna, their fingers gently entwined. She's smiling back up at him from under her vintage cloche hat. There's another slightly blurry photo of them standing behind a boxwood hedge, Bill looking off into the distance with a snappy bow tie at his neck, Anna next to him under the shade of a paper and bamboo parasol. With Anna's dark eyes and Bill's height and light skin, they look like Sazan and me.*

A seed packet of devotion and overcoming the odds, handed down in a few faded snapshots. Heirloom flowers and fruits of a good life.

My uncle, their grandson, who remembers them and knows their story well, told me about an excursion he took with Bill after Anna passed. They'd spent the day shooting guns and exploring Nevada's abandoned silver mines. As they reflected on their day in the desert, Bill sighed and said, "I miss Anya."

That's someone who loved his life and loved his wife. That's someone who lived a very good life.

As you settle in for the night tonight, as you turn toward rest, I want to ask you this: What seed are you sowing for tomorrow? What do you want to plant in the coming morning of your good life? Your answer doesn't have to be complicated or epic. It's a simple evaluation of how

---

* These photos, including one that Sazan and I re-created, are featured on our website: https://stevieandsazan.com/blogs/news/a-generational-love-story.

this day has gone and what you want to carry into tomorrow. You reflect on the blessings of the day you've just lived, and you store the lessons you learned today in preparation for the next day's living. Too often we can blow past what the day has given us as we scramble to put kids to bed, fill the dishwasher, and set the alarm for the night.

But the day has been your schoolhouse. You've learned some things. And often, those lessons can be heirloom seeds for the next generation and the next. When you have an idea of why you lived this day, you can rest well in the knowledge you've acquired. You never know how those lessons might apply. You never know when those seeds might take root. But when you gather them up, the small moments and the big ones, I know you'll see the presence of God in your life. And that's what true rest looks like: knowing there is someone bigger than you who loves you immensely.

Seeds are small. Growth takes time. But harvests can be big. Before you close your eyes tonight, set out a little seed for the coming day. A little good seed, sprinkled in the mixed soil of hard and happy, bears fruit. For your life and beyond.

CHAPTER 15

REST IN SURRENDERING

I (Sazan) had been feeling a little off. Nothing major. Just not quite like myself.

I needed to get more sleep.

But opportunities for rest and sleep were in short supply. Stevie and I were working around the clock on the blog and the YouTube channel. More and more collaboration deals were coming through, and we were always in the process of creating new content. It was an exciting time, but it was also a time that felt unsure. After all, the whole Instagram/ blog/YouTube influencer business was pretty new, not just to us but to all our peers. There was no industry-standard playbook to go by. This was all improv.

We were figuring it out as we went. We'd wonder: *Is it dumb to be trying to buy a house right now? Should one of us get a "real" job just to be safe?* Stevie and I are both prayerful risk-takers, and we both believe in hard work. We knew to keep our heads down, take on as much work as we could, and ask for God's guidance. We had a plan in place for the next few years to really establish ourselves in the Los Angeles influencer business, and to set down roots in a community.

No wonder I was so tired. But I was off by a mile.

Have you ever had one of those days when, in an instant, something hits you with startling clarity? And you can't imagine how you could have missed it once you've had the thought? In the middle of this season, with a contract on a house sitting on our books and a calendar full of work, a realization hit me.

When was my last period? Like, really. Not in a vague *maybe in the last month or so* kind of thing. But rather, *SAZAN! You haven't had a period! In a while!* Sometimes that voice in my head gets pretty loud. And there it was, just like that, an instantaneous: *Woah! I could be pregnant?!*

Now, I have to say, I don't know why this thought was such a shock. For the previous week, I'd been having these extremely vivid, detailed dreams of Stevie and me holding a child and walking into a new chapter of life. But for whatever reason, my nighttime knowledge wasn't connecting with my daytime routine—until the day I realized it had been a hot minute since Aunt Flo had been to visit.

The same day, we had just gotten the news that the house we were trying to buy in Glendale had been appraised, and all lights were green. But in the midst of that happy phone call, I ran a little side errand. I hit up the local drugstore and bought a pregnancy test. *There's no way*, I told myself. We hadn't been trying for a baby. We'd been diligent about taking every precaution. *There is no way.*

Way.

The test immediately popped up as positive. Stevie literally collapsed to the floor. He lay in the middle of the floor of our home, laughing and staring at the ceiling, then going silent and breaking into laughter again. *I think I broke Stevie.*

By the next day, Stevie was crazy excited. He had a whole list of ways he wanted to tell the family. Somewhere in our heads, we had put together a timeline of when things were supposed to happen—and parenthood after just a couple of years of marriage wasn't included on any line of the spreadsheet. But in true Stevie fashion, he embraced God's surprise timing and said it was exactly the right moment for a baby. He couldn't wait to be a dad.

I was thrilled too. Stevie and I both love being part of our big families. We always knew we wanted kids. And we had so many friends who were struggling to get pregnant. We were incredibly grateful that we could even get pregnant, so we didn't take a single second of it for granted.

But this pregnancy would require something of me that I didn't see coming—something that would force me to dig deep into old fears and old ways of thinking. Pregnancy would make me do something I. Did. Not. Like.

. . .

I am a tiny person. Sure, the hair takes up some serious visual space. But my size always seems to surprise people when I get to meet them in real life. The consensus seems to be that I "read" taller on screen. More tall-girl size.

But no. Your girl is short. Pocket-sized.

So when I tell you that pregnancy completely morphed my body, I mean *completely.* While I was still in the first trimester, I could already see my double chin having a field day. I developed the wildest acne, the kind that spreads over your forehead and looks like you've lost a round against poison ivy. By the second trimester, I had these things called capital-*B* Boobs. *Well, hello! Where did you come from? Weren't you supposed to have been around for, I don't know, my puberty instead of knocking on the door now?* I gained over half my body weight during pregnancy. For the people in the back: *over half my body weight.* And there was nowhere for it to go but around. You know those women who don't show for months and months? And then when they do, it's like this perfect little bump appears right on the front of their beautiful figure? *I can't even tell you're pregnant from the back! Look at you!*

Yeah, not me. Because I'm not statuesque, this baby had nowhere to go but bumpin' out. And back. And sideways. Now, don't get all up in arms that I'm not speaking here with body positivity. We've talked through that. What I do know is that I carried that pregnancy . . . everywhere. A first baby would have been a lot of change to deal with and process regardless. But this body change—coupled with the nature of my job—threw something else into the mix.

I'm a beauty and fashion blogger. Though the industry is making some strides when it comes to beauty standards and the representation of various sizes and other differences, it still has a long way to go. And that industry is part of our livelihood, since we collaborate with makeup, hair care, and fashion brands. I spent a good chunk of the pregnancy really concerned about the impact my changing face and body would have on the opportunities we needed for our business.

I've got this, I told myself. *I'll manage this pregnancy. I'll tell it who's boss.* When I tell you I kept myself slathered in cocoa butter for the first half of the pregnancy to ward off stretch marks, I mean *slathered.* Covered. Dipped. Smothered.

Then I got a bad haircut. And I mean *bad.* We were on an influencer trip to the Hamptons, so *bougie, obvi.* I was sixteen weeks pregnant and really struggling. I signed up for a complimentary blowout at a high-end salon in the area. The guy doing my hair asked me if he could clean up my ends a little bit and take out some of the weight. I told him, "Sure!"

Note to self: Next time, make sure "cleaning up ends and taking some of the weight out of one's hair" means the same thing to me and *the person doing my hair.*

He took out some sharp scissors, and in the blink of an eye, I had a new look. And that new look was . . . Edward Scissorhands Meets Korean Boy Band Pop Star. Chunks whacked out of the length. Bits that were longer and bits that were shorter. Weird semi-bangs. Hair every which way. *It's fine, it's fine*, I thought. Then I got back to the house where we were staying, and Stevie got an eyeful. "What's wrong with your hair?" He was startled.

I got myself in front of a mirror where I could do a 360. Yikes upon yikes. It was *bad bad bad*. My hair was my security blanket. Even if my forehead was a pimple patch and my neck was coming in thick, I could at least get my hair to do its thing. But not now.

Not to mention food. I was really trying to stay on top of my nutrition as well, but I was hungry. And hangry. Heck, it wasn't that the baby wanted Flamin' Hot Cheetos and ice cream. *I* did! I didn't want to give in to stretch marks, weight gain, and cravings because I didn't want to lose control of my image. I wanted to keep my hands on the steering wheel at ten and two through this pregnancy.

Surrender is a pretty loaded term to me. Given my Kurdish upbringing, I was raised on the stories of people who refused to surrender to the evil regimes that took their homes, their freedoms, and ultimately their lives.

In my mind, to surrender was to lose. To surrender was to give up.

And me? I'm a fighter. She may be little, but I promise you, *she is spicy.*

I've spent a whole bunch of my life fighting. Fighting prejudice. Fighting to marry my true love. Fighting for my business and my future.

But I didn't picture a time when I would have to fight *myself* so I could receive happiness and contentment and peace. *Hi, my name is*

Sazan. And sometimes I like to not only take the long way around, but also the tough way around . . .

Sometimes we've got to dig in to live a good life. And other times, we have to let go. Pregnancy for me was not only about bringing a new little person into the world, but also about seeing all the ways I'd been trying to hold on to control. Controlling outcomes, my image, and my tendency to perform and to please people. I was worried about being both a good mom and a good businesswoman. I had a million questions about how to organize and manage this new season, but few answers appeared. While I loved being pregnant because I loved this baby girl growing inside of me, I hated myself on certain days for the weight I was putting on and all the physical changes that kept frustrating me, no matter how much cocoa butter I used.

> **Sometimes we've got to dig in to live a good life. And other times, we have to let go.**

Finally, somewhere in the middle of the second trimester, and after many tears and sleepless nights, I surrendered. What my body was doing was remarkable. I just needed to let it do its thing. I had tried frantically to control my body, my time, and my business during this pregnancy, but if I didn't raise the white flag, I would miss out on the beauty, the unique experience, and the goodness.

God was right there to meet me at the point of surrender. He'd been collecting my tears and hearing all my confused, scared prayers. I finally leaned into the way my body was changing. I started eating the dang Cheetos and enjoying them instead of beating myself up about it. I put all the what-ifs on a shelf and answered God's question to me when he met me under that white flag.

"Will you trust me, Sazan?"

Yes.

Something I didn't expect waited on the other side of surrender. First, I realized it takes strength to surrender. Have you ever thought about that? When you're wired to be a fighter, when your superpower is knowing how to dig in, it takes guts to let go. It takes a different kind of courage. I didn't know I could *strongly* surrender. I'd only known the weak kind of surrender—the kind where you don't try, you don't sacrifice, and you give up.

This wasn't giving up. This was going in. Going into the fullness of the whole experience. Opening up to wherever this journey would take me, to whatever my body and my heart would look like afterward.

The other surprising thing on the other side of surrender was the rest I found there. I thought I'd feel guilt or a sense of failure. Instead, I found joy—a spiritual rest from God that I'd been praying for for years. I'd been living in a hustle-and-bustle world for as long as I could remember. But now, I had every reason and then some to find balance in my life, in my body. Surrender entered me into a new fight—one to conquer the culture of frenzy I'd been enduring.

I'm convinced now that the most powerful rest you can experience is when you lay down the need to control. I'd always thought that rest was the reward for a job well done. I thought I'd deserve rest once I'd worn myself out and taken care of all the things. But it turns out that rest is our birthright. It's not earned; it's received. The only way to get there was to surrender all my doubts, insecurities, fears, and struggles to God. Not some of them but all of them. It was incredible to see my life starting to move once I stayed completely still.

> **It turns out that rest is our birthright. It's not earned; it's received.**

·　·　·

So let's answer the burning question on your mind: What about the cocoa butter? Did it stop those stretch marks from forming? Nope. And those marks are a gift. I don't just mean that in a "precious mommy moments" kind of a way. No, there's something way more profound about the stretch marks that now etch my hips and stomach. They are evidence that God used that season to help me shed my old skin of insecurity and fear. They remind me that in order to grow, I have to stretch. I have to leave the old way of doing things behind. God didn't just birth Valentina through the process of my pregnancy; he birthed a new me. He put me in a new skin, one that is pliable and supple to the power of surrender and the value of peace. There's a place where Jesus talks about this very thing. He says, "No one pours new wine into old wineskins. Otherwise, the new wine will burst the skins; the wine will run out and the wineskins will be ruined" (Luke 5:37). What that says to me is that when God is doing something new in your life, he won't try to fit the new into your old way of doing things. You're going to need a new skin to make room for what he's growing in you.

Do you have something you're trying to control? Is it a relationship that isn't moving toward the commitment you crave? What if you surrendered it? Is it a career ambition you've sacrificed for? What would happen if you laid it down? The way I see it, we're all in some stage of pregnancy with something. Maybe you've carried a hope for a long time. Or maybe there's a hurt you keep nestled under your heart. Whatever it is, a wish or a wound, you're trying to manage the outcome. I do the same thing too. Along the way, whatever you're carrying influences how you see yourself. It shows up in what you say to yourself. It impacts how you see your life today, right now. You think: *My life will be good when . . .*

Friend, I'll stand in faith with you for the things you hope to see realized in your life. And I can be a shoulder to cry on when life is unfair. But I also want you to know this.

We can stand, unashamed, under a white flag of surrender together. Because when we get there, it means we've won the battle. We've won the battle against ourselves, against our desperate need for control. And the spoils of that war are there for the taking. Joy. Peace. New life. And rest.

CHAPTER 16

REST IN FREEDOM

The seamstress tailoring my dress chewed me out.

Then the Airbnb double booked us.

Then the weather forecast started PMS-ing.

Welcome to the lead-up to my wedding day.

Throw in a good bit of Kurdish family drama for good measure, and you've got the full flavor.

Okay, let's talk about this seamstress first.

When Stevie proposed, I was ready to get married. Like, yesterday. Do not pass go, do not collect two hundred dollars. We'd waited such a long time to figure out who we were and what we wanted. So when he put a ring on it, I was all, *Let's go!*

That meant I needed to find my dress and fast. But here's the thing about wedding dresses. In a perfect world—you know, the kind where you don't hide your boyfriend from your parents for over three years, a world where you get engaged and take a couple of years to plan a wedding your family will attend—you find your dress. Then the dress shop orders it, and it takes five or six or nine months to come in. Then you have it tailored, and some more time goes by. Then you wear it to your wedding, a year or more after your dress hunt started.

But I wasn't getting married in a perfect world. I was getting married *now*. In five weeks. So I needed something off the rack. I figured I'd get it nipped and tucked and whatever else it needed as quickly as possible.

I found a dress I loved—one I could take right then. Excellent. Sure, it needed to be shortened. And, you know, *adapted* to my frame. Fine. Again, I wasted no time. The bridal store recommended a seamstress, and I got myself over to her pronto.

The first fitting went . . . okay. I wouldn't say the seamstress was thrilled with me or the turnaround time I needed. But I thought we were on pretty good terms.

Until I went back for the second round of fittings by myself.

On that day, let's just say *somebody* hadn't had her Wheaties.

Holy. Moly.

The seamstress yanked the dress around me and started stabbing pins into the bodice. She sighed. Moaned. And generally grumped.

She had dozens of pins in her mouth, anchoring them with her lips. She looked like she held a bank of tiny swords between her teeth, ready to cut and slice.

Which she did, with her words.

"Ridiculous, trying to get a wedding dress tailored this fast!" she fussed, pins flashing from their perch on her lips. "Never seen such a stupid thing!" She kept grabbing handfuls of fabric, wrenching me from side to side. "This material! Ugh! Can't hold a shape. Some of the worst I've worked on!"

I felt my lip start to tremble. This did *not* feel like the dress fitting in a Hallmark movie.

She continued pulling and jerking the hem, the zipper, the waist. I felt like a kindergartner in a bouncy house getting stomped by a sixth grader. "Raise your arm!" *Bounce.* "Turn this way!" *Bounce.*

All that *bouncing* started to make my head hurt.

But she wasn't done yet. Oh no. Not by a long shot.

She spun me again to face her and practically shook me. "What were you thinking? You're supposed to order your dress far ahead of time. You're supposed to reserve several months to work on the alterations! So dumb!" She hustled me out of the dress and pointed to the door of the shop. "Come back in two weeks!"

I found myself dumped on the sidewalk, shell-shocked.

Then I started to cry.

I wanted my mom. My mom would have put that mean alterations lady in her place. *I was supposed to do this with my mom.* It had been part of the dream wedding scenario—a precious mother-daughter moment. But that hadn't happened.

I was out here on my own, trying to avoid getting stabbed to death by hundreds of tiny sewing pins and a razor tongue.

I called Stevie and wailed. I had no doubts about getting married, but I needed someone on my side to assure me the dress was beautiful and that it would all work out. Stevie hadn't seen the dress, of course. I wanted it to be a surprise. But he talked me down and loved me up. He insisted I call my sister to go with me to the next appointment.

That one thing was really incredible during all the wedding drama. My siblings decided to stand by my side. It cost them to do it; they love my parents as much as I do. They didn't want to hurt them. But my parents' stance at that time about Stevie and me wasn't the same as my siblings'. They loved Stevie. They wanted to celebrate us. So our plans included my brother Sherwan walking me down the aisle and my sister Sayran going to the final fitting to block and tackle the seamstress.

Then the Airbnb double booked us.

· · ·

Let me back up in time for a moment. I called Stevie the day after we got engaged, completely panicked. It had just dawned on me that in Kurdish families, the groom's family pays for the wedding. In American families, the bride's family typically pays for the wedding. Every way I could slice it, we were screwed when it came to the financials of a wedding.

"Saz, you gotta calm down," Stevie told me. "Let a guy take at least a seventy-two-hour victory lap after proposing, okay? Let me have a win here for a minute before we start freaking out."

Fine. I gave him the three days. Three days later, I was still freaking out.

"I promise you, I'll figure something out," Stevie assured me. "I'll find the perfect place."

And he did. He had the brilliant idea of booking an Airbnb in Malibu. Gorgeous. Spacious. Views for days. And affordable.

I'm telling you, he's a smart one.

We loved the location and couldn't wait to celebrate with our friends and relatives. We set the wedding for the first Saturday the Airbnb was available and moved forward with the rest of our plans.

Until two weeks before the wedding, when Stevie received a phone call from the person in charge of the bookings.

"So sorry," he said. "But something's come up, and you can't have that particular property."

Um, I'm sorry. What?

182

But there was more.

"And I don't think you're going to have much luck finding anything else on that Saturday. A lot is going on in Malibu that weekend, and everything's booked."

Fan-freaking-tastic. *Saz-panic begins in three . . . two . . . one . . .*

I'm pretty sure Stevie was on the verge as well, but he kept it together. Our perfect Malibu Airbnb with a patio overlooking the ocean where we could say our vows wasn't available on the Saturday we'd set for the wedding, but it was available the day before. It meant we would need to change our wedding to a Friday.

Fine. Whatever.

Dress tailored.

Spot reserved.

Friday instead of Saturday.

The wedding was now just a few days away. Southern California had been in a drought for months, which was why I hadn't really been paying much attention to the weather forecast. It had been the same for weeks and weeks: dry and sunny, dry and sunny.

Then one of those funny little cloud icons popped up on my extended forecast app. *Hmm. That's weird.* Soon it updated to the cloud icon with raindrops, then to the cloud icon with raindrops . . . and lightning.

On Friday?!

Are you kidding me? We're gonna end this multi-monthlong drought on our wedding day? Our OUTDOOR wedding day?

Apparently so. It was supposed to pour.

A couple of days before the wedding, I felt a little tingle on my lip. Sometimes I felt the stress of everything practically oozing out of my pores. But then my immune system got in on the game and popped out one of the most epic cold sores of my life. Right on my lip. Right on the ol' smacker.

Finally, Friday (not Saturday) the Wedding Day arrived.

I arrived early to start getting ready and to check on the cake. Stevie wasn't flying in from his bachelor party until the afternoon.

The rain was coming down in sheets. So Stevie's mom prayed with me that the rain would stop before our ceremony started.

I spackled over the cold sore with some serious concealer. My sisters got me into my dress. I put on my veil. Took it off. Repositioned it. Tried it again. Our people started to arrive. They told me Stevie had made it into town.

And then it was time. Time for me to walk down the aisle.

The clouds cleared. The rain stopped. Our prayers were answered. The sky smiled in a puffy wreath of cotton candy pink.

I locked eyes with Stevie, who stood in the soft sunshine, the ocean thundering behind him.

Step.

That's when I heard it in my soul with that first step. The sound of a chain link falling.

Step.

Another link falling, its echo in my heart.

Step.

And another.

Step.

And another.

With every step I took down that aisle, I could feel the shackles coming off of me. The shackles of doubt. The shackles of hiding my love for Stevie. The shackles of the expectations my culture had placed on me. I remembered the words of Jesus that had been such a comfort to me through the crazy months leading up to the wedding: "Everyone who has left houses or brothers or sisters or father or mother or wife or children or fields for my sake will receive a hundred times as much and will inherit eternal life" (Matthew 19:29).

I never had to lie again.

For twenty-five years, I had hidden behind what I thought I was supposed to do and who I thought I was supposed to be. Now, as I walked toward the man God had for me, I was free.

I was free.

. . .

When you decide to live in freedom, be ready.

Stuff will come for you. And a lot of that stuff will make life feel anything but restful and calm.

There are a million reasons why it can feel easier to just accept the status quo. To keep hiding. To keep lying about what is most important to you and who you really are.

In my case, I wanted all the answers laid out in front of me before stepping into freedom. I wanted to know exactly how this whole thing was going to pan out. I wanted things to line up cleanly.

At first, the obstacles Stevie and I faced with our wedding twisted me with questions. *Are we doing the right thing? Is this some kind of warning? Should we back up?*

Looking back now, it's a whole lot easier to see the pattern—to see the scheme of the Enemy against my soul. Tacks in the road. Family drama. Impossible wedding planning deadlines and all the rest.

> **When you decide to live in freedom, be ready.**

It was all the Enemy's effort to keep me caged in a life that wasn't built on the good, but rather on the gray. Made of the glum, not the glorious. Existing instead of enjoying.

Okay, this makes me mad, but I've still got to say it. That sour seamstress taught me a great lesson about freedom. Had I decided *not* to make that wedding dress mine because of the discomfort that angry seamstress put me through, I could have avoided some bouncing around and mean opinions. The dress still would have served its function. But it wouldn't have been a *fit*.

It wouldn't have felt like my dress.

But I wanted to say yes to *my* dress.

That's what being a prisoner, instead of living in freedom, feels like. It's familiar. It functions. But you're always shape-shifting to suit someone else's opinions. You're molding yourself to what society says you're supposed to be or what's supposed to make you happy. You're lying to other people. And most importantly, you're lying to yourself.

Here's one of the bigger lies I was living: my life was to be endured instead of enjoyed.

Here's another one: I was completely on the hook for making everything in my life work. When you feel like it's all on you instead of God, there's no such thing as rest.

That's the connection between freedom and rest. When you free yourself from the idea that you've got to do it all, when you free yourself from thinking your effort and your stress hold your universe together, you discover freedom.

Freedom and rest are cousins living on the same family tree.

Before our wedding day, I made many things harder than they needed to be. I was stressed about my career. I was freaking out about coming clean with my family about my relationship with Stevie. I thought everything rested on my shoulders and if I didn't micromanage and organize it, it would fall to pieces.

All those links of lies—the ones I was believing and the ones I was living—connected to make a chain. A chain that bound me to living a life that was limited. A life that was *meh*.

Breaking that chain is why I speak so passionately now about the good life. I can look back and see all the ways I was keeping myself from living fully. Sure, our wedding season was full of crazy stuff. Stuff that was big. But I bought into the hype and kept feeding it three meals a day. A breakfast of panic. A lunch of worry. A big dinner of freak-out.

As more wedding details headed toward the ditch, it's a wonder we didn't pack it all up

> **Freedom isn't just a moment. It's a walk. And each step takes you closer to home.**

and quit. But when you're on the road to your destiny, when you're heading toward the thing God has for you, keep going.

Keep going.

Freedom isn't just a moment. It's a walk. And each step takes you closer to home.

. . .

Our friends tell us that as Stevie and I spoke our vows to each other, whales were breaching just offshore behind us. They say there was a rainbow.

I didn't see anything but Stevie.

After our vows, after that first kiss as husband and wife, we headed down to the beach for pictures. Our budget was so tight, we didn't have money to pay our photographer. Jon Volk was there for us anyway. We only had a few minutes of daylight left before the dusky evening turned to night.

The lighting was perfect.

The skies that had held the dark storm clouds now celebrated us with incredible shades of rose and peach. Stevie lifted me in his arms. We laughed. We kissed. We hit a couple of poses. It took maybe five or ten minutes, and then we headed back to the house to eat cake with our people.

Later, those pictures would go viral online. Jon always laughs that his last-minute favor helped launch his career. (And yes, Stevie and I did throw some cash his way once we could afford it.)

We toasted. We cut the cake. We danced in the living room of the Airbnb, the furniture pushed back against the walls. Stevie's mom and dad slow-danced next to us. My siblings and Stevie's cut a rug.

This wasn't just a wedding. This was a declaration. The day was an anthem to freedom, to truth. To courage.*

It wasn't a "perfect" day. I had a giant cold sore, many details went sideways, and my parents weren't there to celebrate with us (although they would eventually).

But it was a perfect day. Because it was good.

After the Wedding

One night, exactly one month after the wedding, Sazan got a phone call from her mom. Her mom asked if Sazan and I could come down to San Diego for a big family gathering over the weekend. It would be the first time I would meet Sazan's mom and extended family. To say I was nervous would be a crazy understatement.

As we got ready to go, I thought about *My Big Fat Greek Wedding* and the character of Ian Miller. When Ian meets all the Greek family members of his girlfriend, Toula, the family has prepared a whole meal made of every kind of meat. But Ian is a vegetarian. Okay, I eat meat (*obviously*, 'cause Texas BBQ), but I wondered if that's how this would feel: white guy me entering a new Kurdish culture and an unknown Kurdish world and unintentionally making it awkward and stepping on toes.

---

* Wondering what that anthem sounded like? The slow dances? The moments that made up our perfect evening? This is the original playlist from our reception, 138 love songs that made up our day: https://spotify .link/1TrTAShxVyb.

The drive down the coast to San Diego from Los Angeles felt both wildly long and too short. When we pulled up in front of Sazan's grandparents' house, everything was quiet. My nerves were pinging close to panic as we each took a deep breath and got out of the car. How was this going to go? How many ways could I screw this up? How many frosty introductions could I endure throughout this day?

And then the front door flew open.

And we were surrounded. Hugs, kisses, tears, laughter.

I was getting *My Big Fat Greek Wedding* in Kurdish style.

We actually did get another wedding, a redo in her grandparents' backyard that night. We were in shorts; it was all impromptu. But when Sazan walked the few short steps to me, we made promises again in front of this new family of mine, and we sealed it by eating from an endless buffet of kabobs, rice, and Saz's grandma's homemade dolmas.

Sazan's family completely surprised me over those two days. I danced with her mom and her uncles around the fire in the backyard, our pinkies locked, while Kurdish music played over the outdoor speakers. I listened to the incredible stories of the family fleeing Kurdistan, desperate to escape the cruelties of Saddam Hussein. And what really set my heart on fire was when all the guys in the family hustled me out to the car and we made a Dairy Queen run for Blizzards. (In Stevie love language, Blizzards are about as top shelf as it gets.)

It's not that everything was fixed in one short weekend. Sazan's relationship with her dad wouldn't find repair for almost three years. There were still plenty of adjustments to be made, and we all had a lot to learn about each other. But over time my relationship with Sazan's family has grown and solidified, because it is a relationship that was forged in the fire of heartbreak and is now cemented in a love that is just as strong as blood. I look at Sazan's sisters as my sisters and her brothers as my brothers. I love her mom and dad as if they were my own. And they are.

• • •

One night a couple of years later, the family gathered together again, as we now often do. Sazan's younger brother and I were determined that we needed to get a fire pit for everyone to sit around. We headed out on a Procure-a-Fire-Pit Mission but came up zeros at Lowe's and Home Depot. We ran into a few more stores, all to no avail. Finally, I remembered the simplest answer to all household and garden needs: Walmart. Walmart has everything on the planet, right? And sure enough, Walmart came in clutch with a fire pit in stock. It wasn't much to speak of, and it wasn't some top-of-the-line model. But we were gonna light that dang fire pit.

We lugged it home and got it put together, feeling like fire-pit heroes. We got that bad boy filled with logs and lit it up. Sazan's family started gathering around the fire. We busted out the hot chocolate and s'mores. The stories started flowing, and the laughter kept getting louder.

And then came a moment. Something I never thought would enter the chat. Sazan's mom turned to me as the conversation and joy grew and said, "Stevie, you really bring all of us together."

To go from feeling like I was responsible for busting a family apart to being told that I was bringing the family together, I still don't think I have the words to explain what that was like. To go from outcast to insider. Enemy to embraced. It was a profound moment of grace.

It's made me realize how important it is to just keep going, to keep doing the right thing, to keep pushing toward those things in your life that seem broken or irreparable. Sometimes what you ultimately find is a way of bringing things back together.

That night made me think about this verse, found in Exodus 14:14: "The LORD will fight for you; you need only to be still." Believe me, resting, being still in the middle of the chaos my relationship with Sazan had caused for her parents, was not a natural state for me. But it showed me that there is more than one way to engage in a battle. I'm so glad that God led me to stand down in those months leading up to the wedding. I'm so glad he gave me compassion for what Sazan's parents were going through, that he gave me an understanding of how hard this all was for them. When I wanted to respond out of frustration, God kept telling me to rest, that he would work it all out.

And he did.

In my own pride and ego, and in my desire to fix things for Sazan, I could have blown the relationship with her parents even further apart.

Make no mistake. The kind of rest God invited me to take on wasn't a static one. It was one in which I had to continually remind myself to stay calm. To be a source of peace for Saz. To actively keep the door of my heart propped open, just in case her parents decided they wanted a relationship with me.

On the other side of that rest, God was at work. That second wedding he orchestrated for us in Saz's grandparents' backyard, it was good. Saz's mom saying that I was bringing the family together, it was very good. From my position of rest, God just kept creating good beyond anything I could have put together through any persuasive speeches or efforts of reconciliation.

After all, he's the God who knows how to create all kinds of good. And then he knows how to rest.

My relationship with Sazan's parents formed out of the kind of freedom that comes from a place of rest: resting in God's wisdom, resting in God's timing. And it's a freedom that continues to mark our bond today. I'm free to be me, they're free to be them. I love them with all my heart, and they love us. And when we're all together, with the food and the noise and the music and the chaos and the laughter, it's one of the sweetest places of rest I know.

CHAPTER 17

REST IN BELIEVING

One night, I (Sazan) got dumped. It felt like rock bottom. But I'd been heading there for a while.

Okay, sure, this may feel a bit like whiplash after telling you about my wedding day and our reconciliation with my parents in the previous chapter. But hang in there with me, because when I think about how to wrap up the journey we've been on together—exploring what it means to live a real good life—this story is an important one.

The most important one.

My life was like a rickety house. I'd built my whole idea of happiness, of what a good life was supposed to look like, on the foundation of emotions, people, and things. When things got hard, when people let me down, or when things didn't go as planned, my world would crash down around me. And, believe me, when your foundation is set on things that are changing all the time, your world comes crashing down on the regular.

Oh, lookee there. It's Thursday. Must be time for my world to crash. Just like it did on Monday.

I was disappointed with life. I'd started classes at the University of North Texas, thinking it was going to be one big party (cue the movie montage of beautiful people having fun). Instead, I was striving so hard to figure out how to be happy. I'd focus on looking as pretty as I could, but a zit could send my day sideways. I'd home in on a friend group, assuming people who seemed to have all the fun would bring me into the land of contentment. But if someone didn't immediately like me, I felt I got left out of a party. My happiness was off the rails again.

Then that nasty breakup happened—the catalyst that brought all my frustration and disappointment to the surface. I realized that nothing I had been doing had satisfied my hunger for genuine joy. My solution was to tell myself there was no such thing as pure joy or happiness. *There*, I thought, dusting off my emotional hands. *That will fix it. If there's no such thing as real happiness or true good, then I can't get hurt again.*

As it turns out, growing cynical doesn't actually make you any happier either. That season of life just got darker for me. I was easily triggered. Quick to anger. Seldom fully present. I found myself pasting on a smile in front of friends and family, when deep down, I felt incredibly lost and confused. I was radically disappointed in myself. Nothing and no one could comfort me. Not my family, not my friends—nothing and no one. I'll never forget the day I was lying on my bedroom floor, feeling like a captive prisoner in my own head, wondering if being dead would make me feel more alive than how I felt in that moment. That was the last thought (and the darkest thought) I had before my life would completely change.

I hated my life, but I couldn't stop living it. I was fed up and knew I was wounded. But I was not weak. I wasn't going to live the rest of my life feeling this way. I didn't have the answers, but I was on a mission to find them. I thought again about my family, about the legacy of my grandparents who had fought for Kurdish independence and for a better life for their children. I remembered that it is in my blood to fight. That gave me enough courage to believe I wasn't born to quit. I wasn't going to quit on my life without a fight.

The changes I made were small at first. I added some new challenges to my daily routine. I added some extra classes to my schedule toward my goal of becoming a news reporter. I started my blog, a creative outlet for my love of fashion, beauty, and travel. I pushed myself to start working at the campus news station.

And that's where I first met Stevie.

There was just *something* about him as we got to know each other— something so pure and joyful. I put aside a lot of the skepticism I'd had about real happiness. Though I had tried to convince myself that real happiness was not a thing, here was this cute guy with bright-blue eyes who genuinely seemed . . . happy. Fun. Excited about life. Yeah, there was something about Stevie I just couldn't put my finger on. But I knew it was real. I sensed depth there.

As our friendship deepened, so did our conversations. He'd come over to chat when I was working on scripts for an upcoming broadcast. We talked about our dreams. We talked about the ambitions we had to become successful TV hosts in Los Angeles. He didn't put the moves on me. He seemed interested in who I was and what I was thinking about. And when I ran into him in the hall one day after having just booked a flight to LA to meet with a television agent, Stevie was wildly excited for me. That's when I began to realize that this was a real friendship, one in which we could authentically cheer each other on.

We got in a habit of sitting in one of our cars, chatting and eating takeout food before heading into the studio or to our next class. Those car conversations, either in my Kia Spectra or Stevie's Chevy Malibu (which had no AC, I might add!), would sometimes go for a couple of hours. The more comfortable I became with our friendship, the more comfortable I felt opening up to him about things that had been going on in my life.

One night, during a car hangout, and after laughing over some silly jokes, I had to ask him: "Why are you so happy?"

He was a little confused at first, but he left me the room to explain where I was going with that question. I told him about the season I'd been walking through, the bad breakup, the identity crisis about life—and I wondered aloud if mine was destined to be disappointing. I told him I felt so lost and just wanted answers.

He didn't try to talk me out of any of it. He didn't give me some kind of pat response, such as, *How can a pretty girl like you think she has a bad life?* No, he listened intently. He took it all in. Then he asked me this question:

"Have you ever prayed?"

"Like, to God?" I questioned.

He nodded. I told him that I had, that from the time I was eight years old, I would chant some basic prayers. I explained that I had a list of things I would run through, asking whoever was out there for help and protection.

His question to me about prayer led me to ask him even more questions. As the weeks passed, I kept hitting him up with all kinds of new ones. He would listen, and he would answer gently. He knew I was searching for something that I couldn't find in this world, in people, in emotions, or in material things. Stevie began to share his personal faith with me. He was never pushy, and he was never judgy. I would just ask another one of my questions, and Stevie would tell me how his faith guided him through emotions and situations. It was the first time

I had ever heard someone talk so intimately about their relationship with God.

After several conversations with Stevie about God, I was very intrigued but still wanted to know more. How could I access this type of happiness and fulfillment—the kind Stevie carried all the time? How could I start a new life? Stevie encouraged me to talk to God myself. "If you want to know the truth," he said, "ask God to reveal himself to you. If he is who he says he is, he will answer your question. Ask the real God, the one true God, to reveal himself in true form."

So that night, with nothing to lose, I simply prayed a nonrehearsed prayer that went something like, "Hey, God. It's me, Sazan. This is kind of weird, and I don't know if you've heard me before. I've been praying to you since I was eight years old, but I'm just wondering if you're even there. Show yourself to me."

That night, in my dreams, I saw myself standing inside what looked like a church. My hands were in the air, praising and worshiping Jesus's name. I'm crying even as I write this because I can still see it so clearly. He was there. For twenty-one years of my life, I didn't know I could have a relationship with God. It was in that season of genuine surrender, of hard questions, of dark times, when I finally opened the door of my heart.

And there he was. Waiting for me. He came for me in my dreams. Jesus was there. He had been standing there waiting for me to open that door my entire life so he could come in, rescue me from a zeroscape planet of despair, and show me the beautiful life I was meant to live—a life I never had to navigate on my own again.

Stevie recently asked me what it felt like in my spirit when Jesus wasn't living in it. What was that like? The best way I could describe it to him was it was like a moon: a desolate place, completely deserted. A place where nothing could thrive or live. A place covered in cracks, tears, and craters from being under constant attack. My spirit felt dead. It was a lonely little place you would never want to live in.

And now?

I'd known Jesus only a short time, but one of the first things he did was to restore my spirit. Today that desolate moonscape looks very different. My spirit looks like an entirely new world that is *alive*. A world that is thriving on everlasting love. A place where now hope, joy, and freedom can live forever. Best of all, I'm not living in it alone anymore. Jesus will live there with me all the days of my life and into eternity.

It's incredible to know that I'm exactly where God wants me—that this is what he has intended for me all along. There's this incredible verse in the book of Acts. The apostle Paul is talking to people who live in Athens, Greece. He's trying to connect with them, letting them know about Jesus and the intention and love God has for them. He says to them,

> The God who made the world and everything in it is the Lord of heaven and earth and does not live in temples built by human hands. And he is not served by human hands, as if he needed anything. Rather, he himself gives everyone life and breath and everything else. From one man he made all the nations, that they should inhabit the whole earth; and he marked out their appointed times in history and the boundaries of their lands. God did this so that they would seek him and perhaps reach out for him and find him, though he is not far from any one of us. "For in him we live and move and have our being." As some of your own poets have said, "We are his offspring." (Acts 17:24–28)

Did you catch that? God knew you would live now, in this era, in this moment in history. On this day. He placed you here. And he did it so you would know to seek him out. Today.

Knowing Jesus doesn't mean life gets easier. I still have days when I'm crying on the bedroom floor. But I'm not alone anymore. Nothing can shake you when your spirit is equipped with the perfect love that can only come from knowing Jesus. He died for me so he could live within me. Within you. Within all of us. God gives us the free will to decide whether we invite him in.

> **God knew you would live now, in this era, in this moment in history. On this day. He placed you here.**

But when you ask for him, he's there.

The structure of my happiness was once built on emotions, people, and other worldly things—and it came crashing down. But guess what? As one of my favorite pastors likes to say, my biggest setback led me to my greatest comeback. Today I have an unshakable foundation that is built on God, his perfect love, and my relationship with him. One of my favorite Bible passages reminds me of the life I have now versus the one I was living before. Jesus says,

> Therefore everyone who hears these words of mine and puts them into practice is like a wise man who built his house on the rock. The rain came down, the streams rose, and the winds blew and beat against that house; yet it did not fall, because it had its foundation on the rock. But everyone who hears these words of mine and does not put them into practice is like a foolish man who built his house on sand. The rain came down, the streams rose, and the winds blew and beat against that house, and it fell with a great crash. (Matthew 7:24–27)

Look, I know a lot of people in our world today think they don't need God. Or they're disappointed with people who say they follow God but who are hurtful or hypocritical. I get it. I really do. But God is bigger than the failures of people. He's bigger than bigotry, deception, and insincerity. I can't talk about the good life without telling you about the God life, the kind of life he has for you if you'll simply open the door. And I want to invite you to take your questions, your doubts, and your anger and ask him to show you truth.

I understand if your culture has steered you away from conversations about God, about Jesus. I grew up in a family where I thought access to this truth was unattainable or not allowed. Regardless of your name, your cultural background, or where you came from, Jesus is available to all who pursue him. Becoming a believer took a lot of courage because so many of my own family members told me not to do it. They were afraid I would forget about my beautiful Kurdish culture and conform to other ways.

> **I can't talk about the good life without telling you about the God life.**

Guess what? You can be Kurdish and Christian. You can embrace and celebrate your earthly heritage while living your eternal one.

Ask him. Ask him to help you with your questions and skepticism. Ask him what it means to be fully alive.

I boldly share this because I can see how God uses unique people to draw us closer to him. He doesn't pick favorites or make you audition. He wants you to come exactly as you are. Know that he so badly wants to walk through this challenge with you. He wants to carry you on his shoulders instead of you carrying so many burdens on yours. Let him lift the weight of your pain, heartache, grief, fear, anxiety, depression, doubt, and insecurity. He can make your life suddenly feel as light as a feather.

For twenty-one years, I looked at life through a blurry lens. Suddenly, everything became sharp. Clear. My life is in focus. My heart is on fire to tell you that Jesus wants you too. Not just part of your life or certain areas.

He wants all of you. Right now and forever.

The good life? It's the God life.

CONCLUSION

BE PRESENT

Here's a fun thing to do. Plan a monthlong trip to Europe, with your kids, in the middle of writing a book.

I knew Stevie, the girls, and I needed some time away, some time to focus on just us. But timing never seems easy, right? New things always pop up. Crises that need to be managed. Medical checkups for the girls. The contractor's schedule for a repair on the house. Work deadlines, contracts, meetings about the book, product launches, and all the rest. Taking off right in the middle of all that life to experience a vacation almost seemed like more stress than it was worth.

But we did it. Stevie kept us moving forward, making all the plans, dealing with my freak-outs over trying to get enough done so we could unplug for a bit. A vacation felt a little irresponsible, and to be honest, I didn't feel like I deserved to walk away from work for a few weeks.

We went back to Switzerland to a place we had traveled to three years before. On that trip, we hadn't had Amari yet, just Teeny. It was incredible to revisit with a new little Hendrix girl in tow, reliving some beautiful moments, creating some new ones.

Toward the end of our time in Switzerland, I was feeling that confusing emotion of being ready to go home while also wanting to stay. You've experienced that kind of feeling, right? I was thinking about how long it would take me to pack while also hoping to hit our favorite spots again before we left. Favorite memories of the trip mixed up with all the things we'd find on our plate when we got home.

On our last morning, we woke the girls, had some breakfast, and headed to our favorite park. The park is called Münster-Plattform in Bern. We'd already been there earlier in the trip, but I knew I wanted to soak it in one more time before heading home. The girls freaking loved this place. A couple of things about Münster-Plattform: Interesting name, granted. From what I can tell, it means "the raised terrace" or "plateau by the cathedral," because it is next to the Cathedral of Bern and it's up on a raised portion of the city. It feels like a rooftop park. Because of its height, it overlooks the city with the most incredible views. Families and kids and young couples in love spend a lot of time there. Little trampolines are built into the ground for the kids. People play boccie ball and have picnics of fresh cheese and bread. Tidy lines of cozy, bright-green benches sit under gorgeous shade trees. There's a little coffee shop near the back where you can get a delicious coffee and a pastry. The place is filled with the chatter of people connecting and catching up, as they overlook the city and the mountains.

There are parks . . . and then there is Münster-Plattform. It's simply incredible.

On this day, the air felt different from the other times we'd been there during our trip. It was crisp and cold, with a snap of chilled spice in the air. It felt like fall was right at our fingertips. We bundled the girls up in their jackets and headed out to the park.

It was pretty quiet at Münster-Plattform that morning. The girls chased each other down the broad sidewalk, Stevie strolling behind. I settled on a bench to watch them, a light breeze sending the leaves of the trees into gentle applause. And in that quiet, in that peace, the bells of the cathedral and the city began to ring.

When you're in Europe, you experience bells ringing during certain times of the day. On the hour. At lunch. But this was different. For some reason, the bells kept ringing, clear tones echoing out over the city. One would chime bright, one would add its deeper voice, and a third would peal in response. They went on and on, joyful and singing, radiant notes ringing in the brisk morning air.

And then I heard something else added to their song.

The laughter of my daughters joined the ringing of the bells.

The same bells that have rung over this city for over six centuries were now singing over me. Over my girls. Over Stevie. Over us.

I felt a flood of feelings move up from my heart to my eyes. I just got so emotional. I really tried hard to hold back my tears, but I couldn't. I went up to Stevie and gulped, "Babe, I'm getting emotional." He wrapped me in his arms. We watched the girls dance and listened to the bells' peals.

As ready as I was to get back home, as chaotic as parts of the trip had been, and as hectic as it had been even prepping to come to this place, this moment felt like a message. God seemed to be telling me, "Job well done. Job completed." He showed me, with the bells marking the time, how to pay attention to this exact moment.

So often in our lives, it's hard to be present. I'm someone who has always romanticized the future. My ambition in my career always kept me thinking ahead. What Stevie and I want to build with our girls, with our family, has also kept my eyes fixed on days to come. Heck, even that glorious morning at Münster-Plattform, I was already hours ahead of where my body was, reminding myself about passports. Trying to figure out how to get nine pounds of Swiss chocolates on the plane.

That tendency of mine to always be nine steps ahead of where I really am, to work harder, to plan further, has helped me get where I am today. But it's also the very thing that could rob me of appreciating and soaking up what all that effort was for.

The bells, the girls' laughter, the crisp air . . . the moment gave me a specific gift.

I came home with the gift of better understanding how to be present. How to be drenched in the heartbeat of right now. When I used to think about taking in the present, I thought I understood the idea. I really did.

But now I *know*.

As I stood there with Stevie, locked in his arms, and as the girls continued to dance and spin with the whole city below us echoing with the ringing of the bells, it happened.

I fell in love.

Hard.

Up to that moment, I had only been "dating" my life. Then I really fell for the present. Fell head over heels in love with it. The *right now*. Not my expectations. Not my *someday*. Not my *when*. I moved from romanticizing what *could be* to falling in love with *what is*. And I'm convinced it's the remaining piece of the puzzle of a good life. To cherish, to embrace, to wholeheartedly wrap your heart around this specific moment in time.

I hadn't encountered this before—the ability to truly see the trip and this sunny morning through my daughters' eyes, through their enthusiasm. Through the beautiful city around me. Through the kind smiles from strangers who call Bern their home. Suddenly a place that was so far away from home started to feel in an unfamiliar and weird kind of way *like* home.

Which it really was, if you think about it. Because the moment you're in, wherever that is, *that is your current home.*

Not every feeling I was feeling in that moment was all sunshine. I felt pure joy, to be sure. There was also sadness over our trip winding up. There was a dash of anxiety about the long travel ahead. There was a splash of panic, of wondering, *How do I keep re-creating this kind of experience?*

All of it was present in this good moment, in this good day.

Maybe you already appreciate your good life, surround yourself with great people, and value who you are. But I want you to level up. It's my prayer you'll believe in a Creator who designed you and loves you right where you are. And that you will *be* right where you are.

It's not easy to stay in the present. So many things try to drag me away from this moment. It's like my mind is always scanning, never locked onto the signal of this tick of the clock. But I'm learning.

> The moment you're in, wherever that is, *that is your current home.*

Right across from Münster-Plattform is an old clock tower. It's called the Zytglogge, and check this: It's been around since the 1200s. What? The tower itself has been a guard tower and a prison, and it became the clock tower when the clock was added in 1405, along with a bell to ring out the time. The bell of that clock tower was one of the ones I heard that morning at Münster-Plattform.

I thought about all the people who have also heard the Zytglogge through the centuries. I can just imagine them, hundreds of years ago, walking through the city. People in a rush. People hoping to get through a day faster. People taking a slow walk with their children to show them the tower. People who were so consumed by what was wrong in their lives, they didn't see the good. People who knew how to celebrate. People who forgot that for every beat of that huge ticking clock, *life* was happening.

The name of the clock tower, Zytglogge, means "time bell." I've been thinking about that a lot. Our good lives are made of days. Those days are made of hours, and those hours are made of minutes. If you look at an old-school clock like the Zytglogge, you'll see these little marks between the hours. Those are called *dashes*.

The moments of this life dash by. We need a bell, not to speed us on to the next thing, but to remind us to pay attention. To soak up this moment. Then the next. And then the next. In sequence. Not rushing ahead and not lingering. To stay right on this dash. Because this minute will dash on by. And so will this day.

In this moment, as we wrap up our time together, that's what I want to leave with you: Don't miss the good life that's with you right now.

> ## This is the bell, right now, that I am ringing over you. It's here. This moment.

It's too easy to look back at the past and think, *The good life is behind me.* Likewise, it's too easy to wait on your good life until the future.

This is the bell, right now, that I am ringing over you. It's here. This moment. I'm sure you've got things you're not too thrilled with in this moment, but I also know there are powerful, beautiful things right now for you.

That's your good life. Yours to surrender to and yours to claim. Right now. And I don't want you to miss a minute of it, your hard and happy and mysterious and powerful good life. You can keep looking to have a good life one day . . . or you can decide that this is day one of your good life.

And I vote that this is your day one.

> I came so they can have real and eternal life, more and better life than they ever dreamed of.
>
> John 10:10 MSG

A REAL GOOD LIFE
PLAYLIST

Scan the QR code to listen to the
soundtrack of our real good life.

ACKNOWLEDGMENTS

It started with a nudge from God in 2018. A nudge that would require us to open our hearts, take a chance, and patiently unfold a message from heaven to earth.

If there's one thing we learned quickly it's that writing a book is harder than we thought and more rewarding than we ever could have imagined. This book would not exist without the experiences and support from some incredible people who we believe God handpicked to help us bring our message to fruition.

First and foremost, to God. We thank our Lord and Savior Jesus Christ for trusting us to write this book and for sharing his secrets with us. He allowed a couple of goofy kids from Texas the opportunity to bridge a gap for people from all walks of life to come as they are and be filled and fueled by the message of cultivating a *real* good life.

To our literary agent, manager, and one of the best humans we know,

Bryan Norman. We'll never forget that rainy day we met in Nashville when you saw something in us that we struggled to see in ourselves. Prior to having you on the team, the direction of this book was totally taking a turn, and it was you who reminded us that we can always begin again. Not only did you hear our hearts' cry but you carried us through this process every step of the way.

Writing a book about the story of your life is a surreal process. We are forever indebted to Julie Carr for her editorial help, keen insight, and ongoing support in bringing our stories to life. Julie, you're the Nancy Meyers of the book world: someone who knows how to shape a chapter into a cozy and intimate experience for the reader. We love you!

To our entire families, starting with our parents: thank you for being the transitional characters who paved the way for us. It is because of your efforts and encouragement that we have a legacy to pass on to our family.

A very special thanks to our two beautiful daughters, Valentina (Teeny) and Amari, who opened our eyes to see how the little everyday moments make up a good life. In the process of writing this book we found out we were pregnant with our third child, a son who we named Oliver after Stevie's great-grandfather William Oliver. You might recognize him as Bill from the story we shared about him in this book.

To all our friends who were the biggest cheerleaders. We were six months pregnant when we shot the cover and couldn't have captured the vision without our dearest best friend and talented photographer, Jon Volk (we love you!).

To the entire HarperCollins Christian Publishing team and the Thomas Nelson group who took a chance on us. Thank you for working alongside us to bring this book and our message to life. We'll never forget that first meeting when the VP of publishing said, "You both have *real* and rare stories to share with the world and everything it takes to write your first trade book." That was the fuel we needed to walk into our book-writing journey with confidence and excitement.

Finally, to our online fam members and followers who are a daily part of our lives. Ten years ago we took a chance on the whole social media thing, and never in a million years could we have imagined what we would harvest through a loyal and loving community. To those we've met and those we haven't yet, we are eternally grateful for the privilege of getting to serve you.

NOTES

Part 1: Morning: Reflect

1. Lemony Snicket, *Horseradish: Bitter Truths You Can't Avoid* (New York: HarperCollins, 2007), 132.

Chapter 1: Reflect on Your Intention

1. Ursula K. Le Guin, *Dancing at the Edge of the World: Thoughts on Words, Women, Places* (New York: Grove Press, 1989), 143.

Chapter 2: Reflect on Your Pace

1. Emily Matchar, "Using Your Heartbeat as a Password," *Smithsonian Magazine*, January 30, 2017, https://www.smithsonianmag.com /innovation/using-your-heartbeat-password-180961952.

Chapter 4: Reflect on What You Say to Yourself

1. Kevin Halloran, "10 Things to Know About Psalm 119," OpenTheBible .org, June 18, 2013, https://openthebible.org/article/10-things-to-know -about-psalm-119.

Part 2: Midday: Focus

1. Israelmore Ayivor, *Become a Better You* (self-pub., 2016), Kindle.
2. *Online Etymology Dictionary*, s.v. "focus," accessed March 1, 2023, https://www.etymonline.com/search?q=focus.

Chapter 5: Focus on Opening Your Eyes to See

1. Stephen Luntz, "The Science of Why This Dress Looks Different Colors to Different People," *IFLScience*, February 27, 2015, https://www.iflscience.com/explaining-perceptions-dress-27387.

Chapter 9: Find Your People and Gather

1. Mark Hyman, "How Social Networks Control Your Health," *DrHyman.com* (blog), January 31, 2012, https://drhyman.com/blog/2012/01/31/how-social-networks-control-your-health.

ABOUT THE
AUTHORS

SAZAN AND STEVIE HENDRIX are globally recognized digital creators who have spent almost a decade in the online space connecting with millions worldwide. Throughout their professional careers, they have been purposeful about inviting people into their lives—one post at a time—to pour more love and joy into their "online fam." While algorithms, platforms, and ventures change, their dedication to kindness and compassion remains steadfast. As true influencers, their impact goes far beyond the digital stage. Both Stevie and Sazan have been brand ambassadors and spokespeople for globally recognized brands including Target, Disney, AMEX, Macy's, and many more. They have been collectively featured in numerous publications, including *Cosmopolitan*, *People*, Forbes.com, and have graced the covers of magazines like *Austin Living* and *Magnify*, to name a few.